SEATTLE

SHADY BEACH, THE AVALON AND EVERYTHING

BIG BANDS AND THE ERA OF SWING

GROWING UP AS A TEENAGER IN
SEATTLE DURING WORLD WAR II

ROGER THOMPSON

1st WORLD
PUBLISHING

SEATTLE

Shady Beach, The Avalon and Everything

ROGER THOMPSON

© Roger Thompson 2010

Published by 1stWorld Publishing
P.O. Box 2211, Fairfield, Iowa 52556
tel: 641-209-5000 • fax: 866-440-5234
web: www.1stworldpublishing.com

First Edition

LCCN: 2010924891
SoftCover ISBN: 978-1-4218-9146-0
HardCover ISBN: 978-1-4218-9147-7
eBook ISBN: 978-1-4218-9148-4

This material has been written and published solely for educational purposes. The author and the publisher shall have neither liability or responsibility to any person or entity with respect to any loss, damage or injury caused or alleged to be caused directly or indirectly by the information contained in this book.

The characters and events described in this text are intended to entertain and teach rather than present an exact factual history of real people or events.

CONTENTS

PREFACE

"It's not where we're going, but what we're doing here in the first place."

—Art Buchwald

I'll be seeing you in all the old familiar places that this heart of mine embraces all day through. In that small café, the park across the way, the children's carousel, the chestnut tree, the wishing well.

—By Sammy Fain & Irving Kahal EMI-ASCAP

I have these moments when I wonder where time and friends have gone. I've grown older, but my thoughts keep returning to earlier times and to the experiences and events that have brought me to where I am today. I find these early events remain much clearer in my mind than events of a year or even a day ago. I believe everyone has some period in their life that is unique and special for them; maybe even worth recording. For me, that period was a few short years spent in high school just as World War II started and ended four years later as the fighting stopped and I graduated. As I went through puberty into adulthood, in spite of the country being at war, these years hold some of my favorite memories, some being unique to the Seattle area. I write this now because I firmly believe that we become more nostalgic with age with a wish to re-visit our youth, and those of us who are lucky enough to live to a ripe old age are able to see earlier events clearer and with a more open mind. The first step in clearing the mind is to take a panorama of one's past and let it gradually slip into perspective.

1910: Japan annexes Korea.

1927: Hirohito declared a God.

1931: Japan occupies Manchuria, invades China & drops from League of Nations.

1937: Glenn Miller's first hit is Sunrise Serenade.

"Of course people don't want war. But after all, it's the leaders of a country who determine the policy, and it's always a simple matter to drag the people along whether it's a democracy, a fascist dictatorship, a parliament or a communist dictatorship. Voice or no voice, people can always be brought to the bidding of the leaders. That is easy. All you have to do is tell them they are being attacked and denounce the pacifists for lack of patriotism, exposing the country to great danger".

—Herman Goring, who established the Nazi Gestapo, at the Nuremberg trials.

9-40: Britain rescues troops at Dunkirk. Hitler tours Paris.

9-40: Italy invades Egypt and takes Somaliland.

11-40: Roosevelt elected to a third term. Hungary & Romania join the Axis.

12-40: Britain takes offensive in North Africa; takes Tobruk.

1940: Seattle's population is at 368,302.

2-41: General Rommel and the Africa Corp. arrive in Africa.

CHAPTER I
RISING CONFLICT

Don't know why, there's no sun up in the sky, stormy weather
since my gal and I ain't together, keeps raining all the time.
Life is bare, gloom and misery everywhere, stormy weather,
just can't get my poor old sole together.

—Arlen & Koekler MCI

In 1940 war meant little to a 13 year old in America. It's hard to comprehend the devastation a war brings unless you find yourself in the midst of a conflict and people near to you are dying. At this time children my age and younger living in China, Poland, Spain and most of Western Europe were learning firsthand about the ravages of war. Both adults and children in America were aware of the wars being fought in Europe and Asia, but were reassured by their leaders that the United States would never become involved. Our country was mired in a deep depression that was at its worst in 1939. In 1932 Germany had been mired in a depression with 43% unemployment, but 3 years after Hitler and the Nazi Party took over they were the only European country with full employment; all due to military buildup. As Shakespeare said in Hamlet; "Madness in great ones should not go unwatched."

As early as 1938 Germany had formed a union with Austria and in

March of 1939 invaded and took over Czechoslovakia. Germany then allied itself with Italy and made a non aggression pact with Russia so that they could invade Poland without interference, which they did in September of 1939. While the United Stated continued to proclaim its neutrality, Britain, France, Australia, New Zealand and Canada declare war on Germany. There was great pressure on President Roosevelt to keep our country neutral, so our country stood by and watched as first Poland fell and then in rapid succession Germany took over Denmark, Belgium, France, Norway and the Netherlands. In July of 1940 German U-Boats started attacking American shipping laden with war supplies for Britain. America's concern mounted and in September of 1940 the Senate passed a bill authorizing a draft. The war continued to spread to Romania, Greece, Egypt and North Africa. In March of 1941 our government passed a bill allowing for lend lease to the Allies and later extending it to Russia. It was termed "lend lease" because the Allies were broke and could no longer pay us for war supplies. We inched further toward involvement when in June of 1941 the United Stated froze all German and Italian assets that were in our country and In August extended the freeze to Japanese assets followed by an oil embargo to all Axis countries. (At this time and throughout the war we produced all our own oil) It took the attack on Pearl Harbor to involve us totally in the war. The manufacture of war materials for us and our allies would start to pull the United States out of its deep depression.

As a thirteen year old, my wars were still between cowboys and Indians or Buck Rogers and the Martians, not between actual people and countries. As the war spread rapidly some Americans perceived the threat to world wide freedom and democracy and so volunteered for the R.A.F. in England or Chennault's Flying Tigers in China. We still stood by as Hitler and Mussolini advanced, always sure in our minds that we were safe from any involvement. As Graham Greene said in the Quiet American, "to be human you have to take sides."

We watched Europe, but did not pay enough attention to Japanese imperialism that had resulted in wars with China, Russia and Manchuria along with the annexation of Korea. Japan lacked the raw materials for an extensive war which these countries could supply. The United States had been sending scrap metal to Japan for years thinking all the time they were turning it into cheap toys; surprise, they turned out instead to be battleships. We were well aware of their military buildup of both land and sea forces, yet our government still failed to perceive Japan as a serious threat. Some of our military men stationed in the Philippines felt otherwise. As detailed in William Maek's book "South to Java" these men stationed in the Philippines had been watching Japans rapid advance down the Malay Peninsula and the buildup of their war ships in the Southwestern Pacific. They felt the next logical step for Japan would be to simultaneously invade the Philippines and attempt to knock out our fleet at Pearl Harbor. Our Governments failure to heed these early warnings led to a near fatal surprise attack by the Japanese fleet on Pearl Harbor early Sunday morning, December 7th, 1941. As President Roosevelt stated that evening in address to the nation, "a day that would live in infamy."

I remember that Sunday morning quite clearly, more clearly than what I did last week. I had ridden my one speed bike to Jakes' corner drug store in the Montlake district of Seattle to purchase the Sunday paper, as ours had not been delivered at its usual time. In the store people were talking excitedly about a bombing attack on a place called Pearl Harbor; where ever that was. At home I relayed the word and we tuned in our one and only radio, something not ordinarily done till after Sunday dinner. It's hard to describe the shock and discouragement of my parents and their friends, knowing that they faced another war so soon.

That peaceful stretch of twenty years would not occur again in my life time. Fear, mostly from the perceived communist threat, would determine our foreign policy for years to come. We would strengthen our military so that we were sure no nation would again catch us unprepared. Even though we were warned by our post war president Dwight Eisenhower of the possible threat from a "military industrial complex" we would allow the military to slowly gain control of our foreign policy and to dominate the countries budget. When a country develops excessive military might they often use force and subterfuge rather than arbitration to settle disputes. Now for over 65 years our deeply religious country has been embroiled in wars, intrigues and efforts to depose or assassinate leaders of countries that do not share our version of "freedom and democracy." In the process we have become the largest purveyor of arms in the world. We have established and now support 750 military bases worldwide. We sell arms indiscriminately, especially to third world countries or those professing to fight communism. This was often regretted later as these same arms would be used against us. The military and arms industry have developed a life of their own. We produce arms we do not need, are soon obsolete and are excessively expensive. In one day the Pentagon now spends 1.9 billion dollars, enough to supply all of Africa with much needed mosquito netting for five years thus helping to eliminate Malaria. (Jeffery Sachs, "Common Wealth") It has become impossible for members of Congress to exert any control over an expanding military complex for fear someone in their district may lose a job. Instead of concern for the country as a whole our leaders can see only as far as their own voting district or campaign contributions from drug companies, health insurers and military suppliers. As Shakespeare said in Julius Caesar; "Who so firm that cannot be seduced?" Obviously not our Congressmen!

In our attempt to patrol the world it has become easier to go to war in little understood countries such as Korea, Viet Nam, Granada, Iraq and Afghanistan rather than resort to diplomacy. While European countries invested in education and health care for their citizens, the United States escalated their military spending to a point where our economy is now financed largely by money borrowed from China and Arabia. The greatest threat to our freedom and democracy seems to have come from within, caused by an overzealous military and a greedy, out of control financial sector. Confucius said, "He who exercises government by means of virtue may be compared to the north polar star, which keeps its place and all stars turn toward it."

5-41: Germany sinks the Hood, Britain sinks the Bismarck. (Tit for tat)

6-41: Allies take Syria & Lebanon: install pro allied government in Iraq.

6-41: Germans attack Russia.

9-41: Germans order all Jews to wear a yellow star: start using gas at Auschwitz.

CHAPTER 2
HOW I GOT HERE?

Somebody loves me, I wonder who, I wonder who it could be.
Somebody loves me, I wish I knew, who she can be worries me.
Cause every girl that passes me I shout "hey maybe",
You were meant to be my loving baby.

—Gershwin, DeSylva, MacDonald—Chappell

My parents first lived in Seattle, had a short stint in Centralia, moved to Tacoma for three years then returned to Seattle where they remained till passing on. I was conceived in Tacoma and rushed to Swedish Hospital in Seattle for my birth. My parents feared that being born in Tacoma would scar my reputation in future years. The only event I recall while in Tacoma is being hit hard on the forehead by a swing seat, which just might explain some of my behavior in later years. My family had rented homes, but in 1934 they purchased their first and next to last Seattle home in the Montlake district. This was a modest residential area located quite close to the city core. The district was bounded on the north by the Montlake Canal which was excavated to connect Lake Washington to Portage Bay, leading eventually to the Ballard locks and so to Puget Sound. The boundary to the south was a wooded boulevard built in earlier days as a gradual bike path to connect central parts of Seattle to recreational areas like

Monlake Home

Leshi on Lake Washington. To the east was the fantastic University of Washington Arboretum, a green belt that was much ahead of its time. Finally to the west was the Montlake playfield and Portage Bay. A streetcar bisected the district and ran either to downtown or North to the University district. A small shopping center on the main street of 24th North was confined mainly to one block on both sides of the street. Not very large, yet it held all the essentials for everyday life without requiring a long trip in the car. There were two drugstores, one on each side of the street at opposite corners; Jamison's and one run by husband and wife, Jake and Fanny Hershberg. The small district held three grocers; Kefauver's was the oldest and family run. The owners lived just two doors from my home. In addition there was a Red and White and a Piggly Wiggly which would later become one of the cities early Safeway stores. There was a bakery on each side of the street, one being a Vandy Kamp's. The two gas stations were next door to each other and in the next block. My family bought all our gas from privately owned and operated Cherbergs. When I first started to drive one still had to hand pump ten gallons of gas into the top glass cylinder and then let it drain into your car's tank. There were two barber shops, one on each side; I went to Bills. Add to this a shoe repair, a small ten cent store, a pet shop, Vic Mix, the handy man, a tavern, a restaurant, a dry cleaner and a movie theater. This was quite typical for a local district during that period. Everything was within walking distance and the grocers delivered at no additional cost. Call your order in the morning and receive it that afternoon. The theater specialized in exotic sounding foreign movies, but succumbed to progress and was converted to apartments. Sadly, the dry cleaner was operated by a Japanese family living in the back of the store with their two children of about my age. When the war started they were probably shipped to Hunt, Idaho with others of Japanese descent.

The tavern bothered my parents no end. They were sure that if a young child were to merely walk by this establishment they could be threatened with alcohol addiction, leading to a life of sin and crime. They were even concerned about my association with my best friend George as his father was known on occasion to partake in a beer at this local establishment. I forgot to tell them about all the time I spent in taverns before and after coming of age. Come to think of it, maybe they were right.

The family and our home 1939 Before World War II

We also had Cunningham's' Ski Shop, one of only two ski shops in Seattle at that time. Mr. Cunningham was also the boy's advisor at Garfield High School, which I would soon attend. He rented very long wood skis with bone breaking bear-claw bindings from his garage, located one door up from the main street. Skiing was not the huge sport that it later became and for those few that did ski it required an early morning train ride to the Milwaukie Ski Bowl at Snoqualmie Pass and a late return to the King Street Station. It was probably the fun and party atmosphere of the train ride more than the actual skiing that appealed to these early skiers.

For Montlake kids, the Arboretum was a savior especially for those of us that were only a block or two away. It was a wide swath of land that ran for over a mile, starting at East Madison Street, passing the walled residential area of Broadmoor and ending where Lake Washington became the Montlake Ship Canal. It contained a windy road for auto traffic, a wide swath of mowable grass that ran the length, thousands of specimen trees and plants, a meandering stream, small ponds and many

walking trails. Much of this land that was closer
to the lake had been marsh, but in the late
1930's Seattle dredged a network of canals thus
creating waterways and islands with the dredged
material. These waterways started around the
back entrance to Broadmoor where their private
golf course and driving range were located. The
canals wound their way out to the Montlake cut
and Lake Washington. As the dredged material
solidified and the water cleared it became a
haven for fish and wildlife as well as teenagers.

My constant Companion
Budge

What better playground could a child ask for? In my pre-girl years my
dog Budge and I spent a majority of our spare time here fishing, swimming and looking for errant golf balls from the Broadmoor driving
range. Budge looked like a cocker spaniel on top, but his wheels were
from a Dachshund, short and bowed. Many of the golf balls from the
driving range would end up in the shallow water or the tall grass. If I
faked a toss in the general direction Budge would assume I had thrown
a ball and looked till he finally found a golf ball. Repeating this would
often produce a dozen or more balls which could then be sold back to
the driving range.

Much of Montlake was built up and down hills as was most of
Seattle, some of which could be quite steep. To make a buck or more
likely fifty cents, most teen boys' mowed lawns, delivered The Saturday
Evening Post or took a Post Intelligencer or Times paper route. Prior to
high school I peddled magazines by bike, having a route that covered the
entire Montlake district. I received a full sized bike on my ninth birthday and it would take several years for my legs to grow long enough to
reach the pedals while seated. My legs finally grew long and this would
be the only bike I would need while young. My father had payed fifteen
dollars for a used bike and had it re-painted bright red in a body shop.
In spite of being only one speed with coaster brakes, it seemed to be
able to go everywhere I wanted. I am sure there were hills I had to walk
up, but most were conquered by just standing hard on the pedals and
pumping. The weight of a bike did not seem as important as how it
appeared. Mine came with white wall balloon tires and I added chrome
fenders, a rear rack and long swoopy chrome handlebars. It took me

everywhere, usually followed by my dog Budge.

In high school I opted for a paper route. I chose the Times as it was delivered in the afternoon after school while the Post Intelligencer was an early morning paper. The few easy flat routes seldom became available, so I settled for Montlake's largest route over the steepest hills. It soon was obvious why no one else chose this route. Most of the houses sat high above the street so that a paper boy had to fold the sheets onto a small square thus allowing him to sail the paper up to the porch, rather like a Frisbee, taking into account wind and side slip. An errant toss required walking up steps with your load, but it did shorten the next toss. It was a must that papers land on the porch and out of the rain for in those days the paper boy also had to collect money at the end of each month and customers could be a little testy and slow to pay if they had been receiving soggy papers. The after school part was not too bad, I even put up with interrupting Saturdays play in mid afternoon, but that early hour on Sundays proved to be a little too much, especially when they came out with those super heavy editions coupled with a rainy morning. Also, collecting meant going out after diner in the dark and rain, often having to return three and four times before getting paid. The times got their money first, I got mine when ever. I stuck with it for a year, but summer appeared and it was time to go to our cabin on Vashon Island. Tough choice.

Cabin on Vashon Island

The Montlake district was an easy walk, maybe one plus mile, from the University of Washington campus, Husky football stadium and the

Hec Edmondson basketball arena. For us, the campus was like another park and playground with expansive lawns, wooded areas, Freshman Pond (named for those that were tossed in for unruly behavior) and great spreading trees to climb. It was still open to the public to walk and drive through unlike now where it is crowded with buildings and one has to pass a security check to enter. On many Saturdays we would walk or ride our bikes to the campus to attend University sponsored educational movies after which we would browse through the Museum checking out artifacts from around the world; especially those Egyptian mummies.

During the football season when the University was having a Saturday home game, a few of us would walk to the stadium early in the morning before the fans or security guards had arrived. The stadium at that time was a one story horseshoe, open to the east end facing Lake Washington and extending into a grassy practice field for several hundred yards. The stadium and the practice field were enclosed by a ten foot high chain link fence with a few rows of barbed wire on top. With no one in sight we could easily scale the fence, hot-foot it to under the grand stands, climb on to the top of one of the restrooms where there was just enough room between roof and seats to hide. We would later melt into the crowd and find a spot to watch the game. If a kid tried that today he would be quickly apprehended and jailed as a possible terrorist.

What was once open space on the Washington campus contains buildings as the University responded to Seattle's burgeoning population and returning war veterans with an ongoing aggressive building program. Even the quirky little nine hole golf course that ran along the edge of the Montlake canal was taken over by the Universities new medical center.

On my birthday in October of 1934 we moved into what would be home till after I had finished college. It was your average middle income home that could be found in any Seattle neighborhood. I never quite understood why my parents chose this home. They probably paid about two to three thousand dollars for the house, but during those depressed times they could have had almost any house in Seattle for the same price. Yet, for a child growing up, the house you live in was secondary to the area and Montlake with the Arboretum and lake access proved to be one of the best districts for me.

The house was wood sided, set back about thirty feet from the street and gave the appearance of being a nice one story dwelling. The front was symmetrical with a central exterior chimney for the fireplace and paneled windows on either side. There was a large entry portico on the right covered with a wisteria vine. On the roof facing the street two arched eyes watched everything that passed by. As one rounded the left side of the house the path descended steeply to stairs leading up to a back porch and then continued down to a small back yard, a garage under the house and stairs leading up to the basement. What was one story in front now became three stories in the back. I can still picture my dad, in one of his "do it yourself modes", hanging fearlessly from this huge wood extension ladder trying to paint the back of the house. He may have been a great baseball player, but he was never the handyman and mother continually nagged at him to hire the work done before he broke his neck. In the center of the small back yard was a twenty foot Sycamore tree, but the dominant feature in back was an immense Maple tree, well over a hundred feet tall, growing right on the south property line. It shaded the entire back yard in the summer making it near impossible to grow anything but moss and weeds. In the winter it unleashed tons of leaves covering ours and all the neighbors' yards and filling our gutters. This would give my father another reason to get out his ladder and risk life and limb. It was so big around at the base and the first branches were so far up that it did not even serve as a good spot for a tree house. Still, it was a sad day when this stately tree came down, but we were all happy to see the sun and it allowed my father to expand his garden; his favorite pastime next to painting the house. It also supplied the fireplace with wood for the next century.

The garage in back was accessed by an unpaved alley that came to an end two doors south because of the steepening land contour. An unpaved drive way led up sharply to our garage. Alleys were common in Seattle at this time as most cars were kept in back of the homes as was the garbage pickup. The few cars plus the heavy trucks using the alley led to immense water filled pot holes. After a few years my father initiated an LID among the twenty homes that backed on to the alley and it was paved along with the drive leading to our garage. The garbage men were always Black as this was one of the few jobs open to them at this time. They would walk up into our back yard to retrieve the cans and then replace them in the same spot! Since the alley dead ended, they had to back out. My dad always left a Christmas gift, usually cigars, on the garbage cans in appreciation of the good service.

The house was heated by a basement furnace that ran on sawdust. If you told people today that you heated a home with sawdust they would just shake their head, but Seattle had innumerable saw mills and tons of surplus sawdust. Some genius came up with a plan to convert sawdust into heat. Our heating system pretty well took up the entire basement. There was a fire box and on top of this sat a four foot high, four sided metal hopper shaped like an inverted pyramid into which the sawdust was dumped. A grate allowed the sawdust to be fed slowly into the fire. A full hopper would burn all day, and it was best not to let it go out as restarting was not easy. The heat was distributed entirely on the principal of heat rising and cold air falling. This required a huge plenum that parceled out the hot air through very large ducts and required even larger ducts to bring the cool air back down. Much of the remaining free area was taken up by a room devoted to sawdust storage, enough to last through the winter. The whole system was a pain, yet it gave out comfortable, moist heat with a pleasant aroma of fresh cut wood. As a child I could never quite figure out why the fire stopped at the grate and did not just continue up the hopper. One of those little mysteries of life.

To feed the monster required a yearly delivery of sawdust from a very large dump truck driven up the back alley, depositing the sawdust on our driveway near the garage door. It then became our job to carry it, one large washtub at a time, through the garage, up a few steps and deposit in the sawdust storage room. It took a lot of sawdust, hence a lot of trips up those stairs, to heat the house all winter! Luckily the appeal of toting sawdust was strong among the neighborhood kids so there was never a shortage of helping hands. The sawdust fired burner was not long for this world and as the increasing uses for oil grew we would succumb to a conversion. This also freed up an immense amount of room in the basement and we replaced the sweet smell of sawdust for that of oil.

Our other antique in the basement was a gas fired water heater that had to be hand lite when ever hot water was needed. One big problem, it also had to be shut off by hand when the need was over. You guessed, it was often easy to forget to turn it off. There were several reported incidents where unattended water heaters exploded right through the roof. I can remember going into the basement after waiting a little too long and the heater is making this rumbling noise and I would debate on reaching for the lever to turn off the gas or running for cover. Conversion to automatic electric relieved much tension and probably extended my and the family's life span.

Had the bombing of Pearl Harbor occurred today it would have been covered on twenty Television channels, twenty four hours a day in living color and on a wide screen. In 1941 we still only had snail news. We had yet to discover the wonders of television and were able to find things to do after dinner other than sitting on the couch, eyes glued on a flickering screen. Information came through the radio which in those days was usually about the size of an icebox (what's that?) and was full of very large glowing tubes. Ours sat in a corner of the living room and was actually built as a piece of furniture. On a good day it could receive three or four stations none of which operated twenty four hours a day. It could cease to function at any time in which case you had to remove all the tubes and take them in for testing to find the errant one. Today's generation will find it hard to believe we were able to make it through an entire day without something stuck in the ear. For kids on weekdays we would usually come in the house about 4 to 5 o'clock in the afternoon to catch the great serial adventures of Jack Armstrong, the Lone Ranger, Batman, the Shadow, the Green Hornet, I love a Mystery or Little Orphan Annie. (And yes, we actually did play outside) You had to eat your Wheaties and drink your Ovaltine so you could then send for your secret decoder pin and so get a heads up on future action. Episodes ran for fifteen minutes with about half the time spent pushing products or a decoder ring, not too much different from today, minus the decoder. Just like with today's soap operas, they ended each episode with a cliff hanger, making it imperative that you tune in tomorrow, but if you owned the decoder you would at least be given a clue. As I approached high school age my interest in the serials waned in favor of more time in the arboretum fishing, swimming and exploring the ponds with Budge. My father had found an old bamboo fly rod in one of the used cars he drove home from work and I became determined to learn the art of fly casting without snapping off the bait.

There was never any conflict as to what we would listen to on the radio like we have when watching T.V. The eight hour day had not yet been invented and men like my father worked the hours necessary to make a living, but he made a point of being home for dinner around six. The radio was turned off; we ate in the dining room with a white table cloth and linen napkins kept in a ring. Dinner was served after we were all seated and we stayed at the table till everyone had finished and we could be excused. If we happened to have company the old rule that children should be seen and not heard applied. I can only imagine the reaction if we tried that today. There were no quickies; meals were served by my father one plate at a time.

While growing up Sunday was still a family day, not only for church and dinner, but for listening to the radio after dinner. Sundays started with dad taking me for my weekly indoctrination at the Episcopal Church on East Denny Way. Early on I looked forward to Sunday school as my father allowed me to sit in his lap and steer the car and later on to even move the floor shifter. He returned home, picked up my mother, drove back to church and exchanged her for me. He took me back home and then returned again to pick up mom. With such a busy driving schedule he never seemed to have time to attend church himself. In spite of all these attempts at lessons, baptism, wine, wafers and holy water I would never be in agreement with any church or their teachings. I like what Dan Brown said in the Davinci Code that "Episcopalians take their religion straight so as not to detract from their misery." My philosophy then and now was to have fun as you only get so many heartbeats and then your toast.

As I became older I took my father's approach and would attend Christmas service with my mother one time a year to sing carols. I even graduated from a Congregational college earning an "A" in a required religion course, but still could not see the logic. Religion's strength seemed to be based on fear and superstition and praying only tries to supplant an individual's ability to solve their own problems. The hypocrisy of religion peaked for me when on March 16, 1968 our

Christian raised troops in Vietnam abused and massacred 504 unarmed women, children and elderly in May Lai. Again during the Iraq war a strongly Judeo-Christian right leaning army that commonly holds group prayers asking for Gods guidance abused prisoners at both Abu-Grab prison and Guantanamo naval base on Cuba. Pascal said, "Men never do evil so completely and cheerfully as when they do it from a religious conviction." If I was to choose a belief it would probably be what the Hindu's refer to as Karma; the idea that we bring on our own rewards or punishments by our own actions or simply put in the teachings of Zen, "each man is his own savior." In defense of religion it does provide some with comfort, joy and a sense of well being. They may even look forward to this life after death, or conversely fear death as Shakespeare said in Hamlet, "the dread of something after death, the undiscovered country from whose bourn no traveler returns."

It was common practice for families to have their main Sunday meal in the middle of the afternoon; after all this was supposed to be a day of rest and reflection and the majority of businesses were closed. It was always an excellent meal, considering meat rationing, and was topped off by home-made deserts. When finished we would all retire to the living room for an evening of comedy, something we appreciated then and could use more of today. The entire country paused for these few hours to listen and laugh at Bob Hope, Fred Allen, Fiber McGee and Molly, Red Skelton, Lum and Abner and Edgar Bergen and Charlie McCarthy. Amos and Andy were so popular that they were on five nights a week and movie theaters had to interrupt the movie and tune into the show. It was said you could walk down any neighborhood street and never miss a word of popular programs. I often listen to old tapes of those shows and while they are a little corny and naïve when compared to todays caustic, mean humor, there was something about just listening that stretched our imagination. We had to visualize Fiber McGee's closet when he opened the door and all his stuff came tumbling out or when Jack Benny descended into his underground vault, guarded by this old man, to retrieve a few bucks. We had to conjure up our own picture of Jack Benny's old Model T or what the characters looked like in Allen's Alley.

I attended Montlake Elementary school through the seventh grade, but then was transferred to Edmond Meany for one year as the city converted to a junior high program. Montlake typified what is great about the neighborhood school. Not more than four or five blocks from any home; a place where you saw your friends every day and were taught by dedicated teachers sincerely interested in the student's welfare; like a large Linus security blanket. The school building was brick, high on a hill with a large dirt playfield. Our P.E. instructor Joe Hagger taught us to play baseball, soccer, dodge ball and on some of those rainy Seattle days, how to dance with girls. What more could a pre-teen student ask for? On the majority of school days most everyone packed a lunch in a brown bag or a lunch bucket and added a carton of milk for three cents. On occasion, if I had earned a few cents during the week, I would head down hill to Jamison's corner drug and treat myself to a fresh pre-package egg salad sandwich and a chocolate milkshake for the tune of about thirty cents. The Pharmacist manned the soda fountain at lunch time, but had a high school girl help out in the afternoon. When he was busy in the back I liked to reach over the counter and squirt a little fizz water in my shake to spice it up.

The streets in many parts of Seattle including Montlake had been paved with special asphalt called macadam. It was black like today's asphalt, but had a very smooth surface which made it excellent for roller skating. It seemed like every kid skated whenever the weather allowed. The skates had to be attached to your shoe sole in front and a strap around the ankles in back. A skate key around the neck was a must as the skates often came off and had to be re-attached. The shoes had to have a thick leather sole for good attachment, but still would become detached resulting in skinned body parts and torn pants knees. It was a treat on occasion to visit the roller rink on Aurora Avenue where they had skates pre- attached to boots.

So it happened early in the morning on December 7th, 1941 that we received the news of a Japanese attack on some base in Hawaii that few even knew existed and fewer yet could have located on a map. That Sunday for the first time we would listen to the radio all day for what little information was available. That night president Roosevelt's speech took the place of comedy and we wondered what was ahead for the country as we declared war on both Japan and the Axis countries.

Newspapers were quick to put out an extra which they only did on other special events like elections or the Lindberg kidnapping. With no T.V. and little radio this was a speedy way to get news to the public. Men and boys would fan out in all the neighborhoods walking down the middle of the street shouting "extra, extra, read all about it, war declared". The times were about to change a little for most and a lot for some. As we entered the war I entered high school and would graduate in 1946, the year the war was over. As I write this we will have been in Iraq over ten years and have not solved much; but then wars seldom do. In some ways we were lucky not to have suffered the devastation that was inflicted on other countries by both the Axis and the Allies. Yet, had we suffered similar damages we may have thought differently about involving ourselves in future wars. We would lose our innocence and honesty and have been unable to find it since. We declared war against the Axis powers which besides Japan and Germany included Italy, Hungary, Romania, Bulgaria, Croatia and Slovakia. We listened on the radio religiously to Edward R. Morrow and Kaltenborn for news of the war's progress. The news papers were full of maps showing ours and the enemies' front lines and troop movements in Europe, North Africa, the Balkans and the South Pacific. Americans had finally found a way to learn geography. My family and I would pay particular attention to these maps after my brother David was sent to Europe to help stem the German advance at Ardennes.

12-41: Pearl Harbor; Nazis reach Moscow; Rommel retreats; we declare war; Japan invades the Philippines, Burma, Borneo, Hong Kong, Guam and Wake Is.

4-21-42: 12,000 Japanese Americans from King County interred inland.

1-42: Japan invades the Solomon's, Gilbert & Marshal Is., Java & Singapore.

2-42: Japan bombs Darwin, Australia & shells an oil refinery in Santa Barbara, CA.

WHERE I CAME FROM:
THE FAMILY TREE

Oh it's a long, long time from May to September, but the days grow short, when you reach September. When the autumn weather turns the leaves to flame and one hasn't got time for the waiting game. Oh, the days dwindle down to a precious few, September, November! And those precious days I'll spend with you,—

—Maxwell Anderson & K. Weill, 1938

My Father - Guy Thompson at U of W

CHAPTER 3
A GREAT GUY

The way you wear your hat, the way you sip your tea, the memory of all that, No, no! They can't take that away from me! The way your smile just beams, the way you sing off key. The way you haunt my dreams, No, no! They can't take that away from me!

—George & Ira Gershwin—ASCAP

My father, Guy William Thompson, was the eldest of five children born in Seattle to Danish emigrant parents. He was the oldest and most industrious of the five and guided the family throughout his long life. His father, Jens William Thompson, had left Denmark for America when only a teenager for he was not the eldest son so could not receive a share of the family farm. He was taken on as a deck hand aboard a sailing ship bound for San Francisco via Cape Horn and Straits of Magellan. He continued north to Seattle where he first settled near Stanwood on Camano Island and would later move to South Seattle, a recent residential area bordering the west side of the Duwamish River, where he remained until his death. We are not sure if his name was actually Thompson or was corrupted by emigration officials due to his lack of English as all our relatives in Denmark go by the name Palmason. After settling in South Park he made arrangements through his family in Denmark to select a girl with whom they felt he would be compatible and arrange for her passage to Seattle. Everyone needs someone they can talk with as there probably were few Dane's in Seattle as early as 1880. The relationship must have been compatible, or at least they knew better than to complain, for they spent their remaining lives working and raising a family in South Park. He worked in a local box factory and later as a carpenter building homes, many of which still stand. He did not believe in idle time, a trait that was passed on to my father and hence to me. He favored work over education an idea that may soon return if the soaring cost of education continues.

My father's education started in a Catholic grade school, not because the family was partial to any religion, but because the school was closer and his father felt the Nuns were better disciplinarians than public school teachers. His stay at the Catholic school was short lived as one day during a baseball game on the school grounds Dad drove a ball through one of the schools windows. He did not stay around to hear what the Nuns had to say to him, but took off running. In spite of some small inconvenience, from that time on he only attended public schools.

It's difficult to look at South Park today and picture it as a residential area as it is almost entirely industrial. This would have been rural in my father's day, lightly populated with homes and small farms and nestled right on a big bend of the Duwamish River. Indians still paddled up the river to trade and unless you had a canoe or a row boat, your only access to greater Seattle was a bridge at first avenue south. When my father was young the Duwamish was made up of the Black River flowing out of the south end of Lake Washington and the Green River starting in the Cascade Mountains. Until 1916 when Lake Washington was lowered nine feet, it was very popular to canoe from Elliot Bay into the Lake or continue on up the Green River. After the lake was lowered the Black River ceased to exist. Following the window incident my father went on to Homer Elementary and then to Broadway High school, which opened in the fall of 1902, as he has a few orange and black "B's" in his scrapbook. Neither school was easy to get to from South Park and Dad said that he rode a horse to school at times, but I am not sure how often. More than likely he went mainly on foot.

It was not only the Duwamish that made getting around difficult, but Seattle had plenty of rain and you could pretty well count on a number of heavy snow falls in the winter. People like my father were able to cope with adverse conditions as he would make it through high school and made sure his brothers and sister did the same. He was never much of a student, but turned out to be a heck of a baseball player as were two of his brothers. This helped to keep them in the education system. Dads' father was not a great believer in higher education and felt an able bodied boy should learn a trade as soon in life as possible. This was common at the time and only a small percentage of children ever went on to college. My father received little encouragement to even finish high school and no assistance in attending college. It was lucky my dad went to college for other than catching a baseball, he was always poor with his hands and unlike his father would have made a second rate carpenter.

The beautiful summers made up for those tough winters. The Seattle my father grew up in, especially in the summer, bears little resemblance to Seattle today. Seattleites' like to think of themselves as outdoor types because we have a lot of boats and people ski and bike some. These early residents lived for the outdoors. As early as 1902 Alki beach, which is Indian for "in a while", would have as many as 2000 campers on a summer weekend. The beach would be full of tents, bathhouses and refreshments. Up to 1917, for 5 cents, you could take a ferry from down town to Alki beach where people actually swam in the sound or in the huge salt water Natatorium. That's hardy!!

A cable car ran all the way from town, up Yesler Street, to the top of the hill overlooking Lake Washington at Leschi, all in 16 minutes, leaving a short walk down hill to the beach. In addition, as early as 1897 the city was building easily graded bike trails that ran up to the north end of Capital Hill and then meandered down to the lake and Leschi via what is now Lake Washington Boulevard. Most of the trail became streets except for Interlaken Boulevard at the north end of Capitol Hill. Leschi, or as it was often called Flea burg, was Seattle's fair weather resort. It held the Leschi Pavilion built out over the water; home to dances, romances and stage shows. There also was a large boat house extending over the water that rented canoes, not motor boats, for transportation. There was the Lake Washington Hotel and Restaurant, and one could catch a ferry for Mercer Island or Bellevue or one of the passenger only Mosquito fleet to other spots around the lake. A Mosquito fleet also visited almost all the small towns that fronted on Puget Sound. With an increase in cars, highways and bridges it all came to an end. The last ferry to Kirkland along with the lakes last Mosquito boat was 1950. Too bad, it would have been quicker than waiting 30 to 45 minutes to get across one of the floating bridges.

In 1900 when dad was about 12 years old Seattle's population was a little over 80,000, by 1910 it was 237,194 and growing fast. By 1930 it had reached 365,583, but was slowed by the depression and by 1940 the city had added only about 3000 more people. As the city grew it developed a great transportation system on both land and water. The inter urban rail lines ran south to Tacoma (1905) and north to Everett (1902) and were electric, using a third rail out of town and an over head line in town. In Seattle they taught children the 4 R's; reading, riting, rithmatic and third rail. It took 75 minutes to reach Tacoma at 60 MPH maximum speed. It cost all of 60 cents, but for 25 cents more one could have your own parlor car. By 1919 they would carry three million passengers a year; then came the proliferation of the Ford Model T and A's followed by Highway 99 to the south and Aurora to the north. Much to our regret in later years, the Seattle-Tacoma line saw its last car on December 30, 1928.

When one lives for nearly 100 years you see a lot of changes no matter where you are. My father saw the city tear down the hills surrounding the central waterfront and dump 10,000 cubic yards of dirt a day into Elliot Bay; so much that ships ran aground on the fill. This would upset down town from 1906 to 1929 when they finally finished 5th Avenue. He saw them dig a ditch from Lake Washington to Puget Sound; build the Ballard Locks and the ship canal. The first summer cabin he would rent was in Bellevue, on Meydenbauer Bay, now one of the state's largest cities. Maybe, as he watched all the changes taking place he saw his future with the automobile and not with his degree in journalism.

When looking at my father's early life I do have to wonder how he was able to accomplish so much with little or no help. It may have been his willingness to put in the long hours. It seems he always had some sort of a job, full time in summer and part time during high school and college. Yet in the four years he was at the University of Washington he was able to letter in baseball all four years. He joined Theta Delta Chi fraternity which gave him a place to live, avoiding a commute from South Park. During one summer he helped survey the Cedar River water shed, source of Seattle's water supply. In summers he also found time to play semi-pro baseball for one of the small towns around Seattle. Towns around Puget Sound such as Port Gamble, Winslow, or Enumclaw would all have a ball team and the competition was fierce. In 1913 his Port Gamble team were the Northwest Champions. Baseball along with the beaches and the multitude of lakes that surround Seattle was Seattle's summer entertainment and it was all outside. Dad and all the team played because they loved the game, receiving only their uniform and transportation expenses.

As if that wasn't enough, he also found time for girls and a full social life. I have his scrapbook he kept while in College and it's full of dance programs from his fraternity, several sororities, a dance club he belonged to called the Fussers and all sort of other school functions. From perusing his scrap book it would seem he never missed a chance to go dancing and the programs were all full so he never sat out many dances. His social life did not pause come summer. He used to talk about the big dance hall at Leschi and others at small lakes like Angle, Beaver and Wilderness. A couple could also catch one of the many small steamers that plied Puget Sound and go to Indianola on the Kitsap Peninsula where there was not only a dance hall, but miles of warm sandy beach laden with clams. I don't know how he did it, but he sampled everything. His love for dancing extended on into his married life where he and my mother would belong to a dance club well into their sixties.

So, in review, my father belonged to the dance club Fussers, the Rooters which helped arouse team support, the Oval club for outstanding athletes and the Cadets, a precursor to R.O.T.C... He was able to accompany his baseball team to Japan on an ocean liner where they played one game in Osaka, one in Kyoto and ten in Tokyo. Upwards of 15,000 would attend each of these games. In his last year in school he was the team captain. He even found time to sail to Victoria for a weekend. He must have dated a number of different girls as he has dance programs from the Chi Omega, Pi Beta Phi and Alpha Tau Omega sororities. He lived at the fraternity during the school year paying his own bill, but the receipts show he was often in arrears. What made it all possible was that things were less expensive and there was little to no inflation like we have today. Room and board for the fraternity stayed about$4.50 a month. If you took you girl out to eat after the dance this is what it might cost: Sandwich, 10-15 cents, soup, 15 cents, salad 20-25 cents, milk shake 10 cents, Sundae 10-20 cents and a soda 5 cents. This was around 1916, but there was very little difference 30 years later when I was in my teens. Now days we feel that with only two or three percent inflation a year we're in great shape. Inflation is good for big business and corporations, but not so good for the working man who is always trying to catch up.

Most of Dad's fingers were slightly bent or misshapen from years of baseball. The early gloves they used were not much larger than the player's hand and were not well padded. There was no foot long hunk of webbing to help snag the ball, instead the ball was caught in the palm of the hand, often resulting in bruised or broken fingers. I never thought of him as having the agility or swiftness needed for playing baseball; however I was not around during the height of his ball playing years. Even in his 40's and 50's when we frequently played catch, he had the touch and handled the ball with ease.

Sometime during dad's college days he and two of his brothers discovered the game of golf. He played at the public links on occasional weekends or whenever he was not busy selling cars. He played with my brother David and allowed me to tag along starting at the age of six or seven. The clubs he used had wooden shafts and odd names like Mashie, Nib Lick and Brassie instead of numbers. It was easy to walk the course and carry your bag as it only contained about six or seven clubs. I would be allowed to hit a ball of my own once we were off the tee and so over the years became a mediocre player and continued playing for many years. We played this way until I started to spend summers on Vashon Island.

My father was nice appearing, but not what one would call handsome. He stood about 5'11" with a rather large head and nose and ears.

He was not fat, but had a stout appearance and a slight pot belly. He loved his gardening, but was never much of a handyman, probably due to his misshapen fingers. He was not what I would term a funny person, never telling jokes, but he was honest, good humored, very sociable and well liked by all who knew him. He graduated from the University of Washington in journalism, but worked at it only a short time. I saw some of his grades and there were few above a C, but as mentioned before he led a full life while in college. What he lacked in academia he made up for with an industrious bent and never seemed to tire out. Out of college he was able to send two of his brothers through a two year dental school in Portland, Oregon. Because he grew up with little outside help he was quick to offer aid to good men who were down on their luck. He often extended small loans to men he felt were honest and hard working just to help them over a rough period. Unusual for this period, the loans were sometimes to Blacks. He told me once that he had never lost a dime on these loans.

Mother and Father
Wedding Day San Diego

As with many young men at this time, his life would be interrupted by World War I. Close to being drafted he chose instead to sign up for the newly formed air force and was sent to San Diego for training. He was lucky in several ways. Because he signed during the latter part of the war and never got to fly in one of those early temperamental aircraft, for the armistice was signed shortly after his arrival in San Diego. Secondly, he met a lovely girl named Ruth Paine from Glencoe Minnesota who happened to be staying with her sister Lettie. Lettie had come to southern California for the only known treatment at that time for tuberculosis; rest and cold dry mountain air. The treatment had been successful and Lettie had decided to make San Diego her permanent home rather than return to those cold Minnesota winters. It was a whirl-wind romance and dad must have done some fancy talking for he was able to not only convince Ruth to marry him, but to return with him to a far northern outpost full of rain, wild Indians and little or no culture. She was, after all, the daughter of a prominent Minnesota banker and was accustomed to the finer comforts of life. My father had no home and no prospect of employment. No problem, love would conquer all. It turned out to be one of those perfect unions seldom seen today and they would remain happily married for over 75 years. In those years I would never hear either one say a mean word to the other. They had disagreements, but never continued to hold a grudge. I think it helped that my father was always smart enough in giving mother the final word.

For a short time, after returning to Seattle, my father followed his vocation in journalism by accepting the position of editor on a small newspaper in Chehalis Washington. But due to his interest in the rapidly increased use of the automobile, his stay in Chehalis was short. He started selling Fords for Burt Blange near downtown Seattle, doing so well that he was asked to run a branch agency in Tacoma. He had found his niche in life and would remain a car salesman in Seattle until retiring at the age of 86. Part of the reason he was successful was his extreme honesty, always making sure that his customers were 100% satisfied. This made buyers want to return when they needed a newer car. The other reason was that he was willing to work six and seven day weeks, always thinking of new ways to find customers, but never becoming pushy. It could not have been easy selling cars during the depression years. To find buyers he would often drive out to the small surrounding towns like Black Diamond or to the truck farmers along the Duwamish River and show a car to men those that were still working. He would set up on a corner with his car and talk to anyone that happened by, a trait he never lost. My mother usually tagged along and waited in the car. I know she would take a long soak in a very hot tub before leaving to help her stay warm as she waited, for the early cars seldom had heaters.

In the mid 30's my father decided to strike out on his own and took over a Dodge and Plymouth agency in rapidly developing Renton just south of Seattle, but the depression continued to get worse and he decided to abandon the dealership in favor of working for the S.L. Savidge Dodge and Plymouth agency on Broadway. He stayed with Savidge, selling new and used cars, till his retirement. Maybe, if he had known that the war would rescue the economy from the depression he would have kept the Renton agency, but then we probably would have relocated and all the things that I now write about would not have happened. It shows again how small events shape people's lives.

The key to his success lay in repeat customers and the fact that he really enjoyed selling. He was offered the manager position at S .L. Savidge several times, but refused in favor of remaining a salesman. I am convinced that people really did not care which car they bought, as all cars are fairly similar, but they would seek out the salesman that was honest, not pushy and made them feel important. That was my dad. He received recognition one year by being voted Seattle's outstanding salesman of the year, an award he earned and well deserved.

His trademark was a half chewed cigar and a fedora on his head. When I picture him in my mind it is always with a Vandyke clenched between his teeth. He was not alone in the smoking of cigars; all his friends socially and at work smoked or chewed them almost all day. Tobacco in some form was a national habit. My basic gifts for him at Christmas were a crazy tie and a box of Vandyke's, his favorite. A tie because he always wore a dress shirt, a suit and a hat for work. I remember one time, at about the age of eighty and on the advice from his doctor, he tried to stop smoking. This turned out to be much harder on him and us than the smoking and the doctor finally advised him to resume smoking before he drove himself and those around him nuts. If he had stopped he may have lived to a hundred rather than just ninety nine.

As I've said, he had the gift of gab. It made no difference where he was; at the ball park, standing in line at Manning's for dinner or waiting for the ferry to take us to Vashon Island, for it would not be long before he had struck up a conversation with someone. Talking to strangers would irk my mother, but this was a part of his charm. Besides being honest he was very even tempered, though I would test this temper at times as I tended to be a little sassy and did not always mind. He used a type of razor that could be re-sharpened on a long leather strap which served a dual purpose if I became too obstreperous. As dad applied the strap to my butt, mother would always say, "This hurts us more than it does you"; like hell it does. I can remember only one time when he really lost control and tried to kick me down the basement stairs. Sensing imminent danger I took the first five stairs in one jump thus avoiding a head plant on the cement floor.

Politically, he would remain a staunch Republican. Of course kids always support their parent's convictions, especially when they are in grade school and high school. Some are not able to escape their parents influence and enter adulthood with no opinions of their own. He felt that anyone willing to work could find a job and "lift himself up by his own boot straps", a term he often used. He did not approve of the government sponsored work programs such as WPA (Works Progress Administration) or the CCC (Civilian Conservation Corp) as a means of having un-employed men do useful work while also helping our country. His picture of a WPA worker was always a man dozing while leaning on his shovel. In reality these men did incredible work building and maintaining our national parks, especially in the west. The three million men in the CCC would plant an incredible three billion trees and make thousands of miles of trails through our parks. The WPA was full of talented men that would build beautiful, unique lodges that are still in use today. The men were paid $25.00 a month; could keep only $5.00, sending the rest home to help their families. Workers were encouraged to take courses in their spare time to complete high school and could take college extension courses. On their days off the men would all load into the work trucks and drive to the nearest town for a dance or to buy their cigarettes at 10 cents a pack. These men are the ones who worked on the TVA (Tennessee Valley Authority) for flood control that would eventually be the start of rural electrification. They would clean up the eastern swamps that would lead to the eradication of malaria in the United States. These programs, though often criticized, created thousands of jobs and gave men hope while investing in our countries infrastructure. They came in as boys and left as men. Just like today, the wealthy wanted the income tax reduced as the correct way to stimulate the economy. I could see my father's opinion altering in later years after he and my mother had the opportunity to visit many of the magnificent lodges in our national parks.

As with many who continue in higher education, my thinking tended to become more liberal. We see that large corporations and businesses are seldom run for the benefit of the public and our government often leads the country into situations that are damaging to the populous. It was during the Vietnam War that my father and I had a real parting of the ways. We had never really argued politics much before this even though he knew I had a liberal bent. These would be our only heated discussions as I was very anti-war and he felt we should win the war at any cost. I remain to this day a critic of a government foreign policy that was based in the 1950's, 60's and 70's on the fear of communist expansion and now on the competition for middle east oil and a fear of the Taliban.

1-42: U.S. forces arrive in Britain; German U-Boats off our coast; Rommel attacks.

3-42: 12,000 interned Japanese join the U.S. military. Not mixed with Caucasians.

4-42: 76,000 U.S. men surrender at Bataan; 5,000 die on "death march".

4-42: General Doolittle's B-26 raid on Tokyo from the carrier Hornet.

CHAPTER 4
DEAR RUTH

Day by day I'm falling more and more in love with you and day by day my love seems to grow. There isn't any end to my devotion, it's deeper dear by far than any ocean. I find that day by day------
—Weston, Stordahl & Cahn—FMC

My mother, Ruth Marance' Paine, was born in 1888 in Glencoe Minnesota. Her father was a prominent local banker and helped establish branches in both Glencoe and nearby Bird Island. My mother was proud of the family roots. A complete search had been done by one of her cousins while he was a member of the diplomatic corp. stationed in Ireland. The Paine ancestry was traced back to Jonathan Brewster who came to the Plymouth Colony on the "Fortune" in 1621. The Paine name originated when Benjamin Brewster, son of Jonathan, married Anne Addis and through successive generations led to Seth Paine, a Minute Man during the revolution, living then in Lebanon Conn. In 1797 Seth and his son Thomas Paine left Lebanon, Conn. And traveled for thirteen days to reach German Flats in upstate New York and became the first settlers of Paines' Hollow, N.Y. Seth married Jerusha Swift as her family had also move to Paines' Hollow. Their son, Philander Alonzo Paine moved west with his wife

Sally Filkins, rafting down the Ohio River, and settling in Sand Springs, Iowa in 1867. Their son, Thomas Monroe Paine, moved on with his wife, Anna Marance' Donohue to become a banker in Glencoe Minnesota. We do not know as much about the Donohue line except that her ancestors of the Donohue Clan are buried at the Muckrose Abby in Ireland. So much for genealogy, it can become very complicated.

There were three sisters; Ruth, Olive and Lettie, names seldom seen now. A fourth sister died in infancy. She was raised in one of the largest homes in Glencoe complete with hired help to do all the real work like gardening, cooking and house cleaning. Even though well-off, indoor plumbing was years away and they depended on an outhouse, but very fancy, with a covered arbor extending out from the back kitchen door to protect those in need from the Minnesota cold. It probably did not help in keeping one's bum warm. Of course no one ventured to the outhouse at night, so chamber pots were used and emptied in the morning by the help. This large a house took a lot care and attention which was done by workers my mother liked to call "Bohemians". They were actually men and women hired from the surrounding farms and were mostly Scandinavians earning extra money working for the townies.

My Mothers home in Glencoe, Minn.

The house was two stories plus an attic for storage. It contained five bedrooms, a parlor, living room, dining room and a large kitchen-pantry with a wood stove for both heat and cooking. Lighting was by gas lamp, but was later replaced by electricity. The rest of the house was heated by three large cast iron, coal fired stoves that were removed at the start of each summer, cleaned and stored in the shed till needed the next winter. There was a crawl space that allowed access under the house. This entailed banking the sides of the house with straw and dirt in the winter to prevent frozen pipes. It was all cleared away again in the spring by; you guessed it, those same "Bohemians". The house was situated on a whole block with deciduous trees that helped cool it in the summer. A house like this would not have been possible to maintain without outside help.

My Mother in College at Hamlin

Mother was the youngest of the three sisters and the only one to continue on to college. Her father Thomas Monroe Paine and mother, Anna Marance' Donohue Paine were not 100% in agreement with the idea of women seeking higher education, but in the end relented and went along with it mainly because mother was a superior student and very well read for her time. She attended Hamlin College in Saint Paul Minnesota, joined a sorority where she lived during the school year and received her teaching certificate. She must have enjoyed the college experience as her education continued for four to five years. Upon graduation she accepted a position teaching high school in the northern "Paul Bunyan" country of Bemidji Minnesota. This worried her father as he looked upon Bemidji as being nothing more than a northern outpost. Even though mother was small, being only 5'3", she was determined and would not be dissuaded from accepting the position. It was, though, quite different from what she had expected. These "Bohemians" seemed huge and at first she was a little frightened and as winter approached it turned much colder than what she was accustomed to in Glencoe. She was small of stature, but kind, patient and considerate; qualities these large students came to appreciate. Her teaching career ended during the second year when word came that her sister Lettie had contracted tuberculosis and their father had decided to send Lettie to the high mountains east of San Diego. To show their appreciation for her kindness, the whole school and much of the town came to the station to say goodbye.

Anut Lettie

Just like in Thomas Mann's book, "Magic Mountain", cool, dry mountain air was the only known approach to TB at that time. It was decided that my mother should travel with Lettie and remain in the area the several years it would take to exact a cure. Lettie was cured, but lost her fiancé who chose to marry another rather than wait; his loss. Lettie would never marry or return to Glencoe; instead choosing to remain in the mild Southern California climate. She bought a home where she lived with her mother. After the death of her mother she moved to an apartment overlooking the San Diego city center. Because Lettie had been ill for so long and had never acquired any work skills her father left her a fair sum of money allowing her to live comfortably and even travel some in Europe. As interest rates fell after World War II her income dwindled and she was forced to move in with me and my parents where she lived out the remainder of her life. We were the lucky ones. Without a doubt, she was my favorite woman other than my mother. Lettie was tall and statuesque, nearly six feet, kind, considerate and soft spoken; one of the last true ladies.

Aunt Letties Great Home in SanDiego

When my mother and father first came to Seattle they rented an apartment across the street from the dance pavilion extending over Lake Washington. I can only imagine that this is where they first became accustomed to dancing with each other. When they finally settled down in Montlake after several moves, mother would have little trouble carving out a niche for herself in what she had feared would be the Wild West. She was smart, soft spoken and well read. She made friends quickly and kept them for life. She managed to keep track of and write to all her extended family; some in Minnesota, Indiana, Wyoming and California. She found outlets for her intellect through the Antiquarian Society, a book club and bridge and dance clubs. She was a voracious reader which soon led to her being in constant demand to give book reviews.

Mother's concessions to living in Seattle were; help with the house work and ironing once a week from Mrs. Dodge and once a week dressing up and dining out on a white table cloth. There were few restaurants that met the description at that time. Her favorites were The Pine Tree Inn and The Hearthstone, both located on the mezzanine of downtown office buildings. My problem was I had to dress up like little Lord Fauntleroy and neither one served hamburgers. My restaurant of choice, seldom allowed, was Hesses' on the corner of Broadway and Olive way, one of the few restaurants to specialize in hamburgers. The Triple XXX drive in chain I frequented in my teen years served great burgers, but was not an ideal place for the family.

Mrs. Dodge cleaned the homes and baby sat for several families in Montlake. She and her husband were of Dutch decent and while she cleaned homes, he worked a Boeing. To me she was quite unusual; very short and stocky with a grumpy looking face that kept me in doubt as to her mood. I likened her to one of the seven dwarfs. In spite of her gruff appearance she was extremely kind hearted, but firm and never took crap from any of the kids she cared for. I am sure we were all a little afraid of her; I know I was, so no one risked giving her a bad time. My parents looked upon her as a miracle worker as she was not only good at cleaning and ironing, but could make kids behave.

Mothers' life in Seattle may not have been as elegant as what she was accustomed to; growing up as the daughter of a banker, but she always kept a nice home and was married to a hard working man who never stopped loving her. Despite those depression years and the following war, if mother felt something was a necessity, father would always find a way to make it happen. She remained frugal and understood the limitations of the times, never nagging. Even with money being scarce the few cloths she carefully selected were purchased from either I. Magnum or Fredrick and Nelson and then only by appointment and always from the same sales girls. Like many people of that generation, she believed in loyalty, a trait that has since been lost. We bought our groceries at the local Red and White market and our meat right next door from the local butcher who cut it up or ground it while you watched; no E coli here. We frequented the local bakery, the barber, gas station and shoe repair. These people gave excellent service, but also became our friends and were often our neighbors.

The friends my parents made in both Tacoma and Seattle they kept for life and added many more as the years passed. My mother would out live them all, finally passing away quietly in a nursing home near Kirkland at slightly over the age of 100. Her health was not really poor and her mind was still keen, but she felt tired, having out lived dad, and felt she had lived long enough. Due to her strong Christian beliefs, had the "death with dignity" law been available I doubt she would have chosen that way to go. My father had passed on about a year earlier at this same rest home and she was truly alone. My brother and I visited her often, but it's just not the same as living with a loved one. The Chinese have the correct answer to old age, no retirement homes there. At least she and dad had been able to live together for over 75 years. We had stayed close as a family all during their life time, as both my brother David and I remained and worked in the Seattle area; me in Ballard and David in Bellevue. A week never went by that I did not visit my parents two or three times. When one has remained that close with your parents over so many years, separation becomes extremely difficult. I know everyone thinks their mother is the kindest, gentlest, most intelligent person in the world, the difference, mine really was!

5-42: First Allied 1,000 bomber raid on Germany at Cologne.

6-42: First mass murder of Jews at Auschwitz; Rommel Takes Tobruk.

6-42: Eisenhower arrives in Britain; Rommel advances to El Alamein.

11-42: U.S. troops invade N. Africa; Rommel starts to withdraw.

CHAPTER 5
DEPRESSING TIMES

Once I built a railroad, made it run, made it race against
time.
Once I built a tower to the sun, brick and rivet and lime.
Once I built a tower, now it's done, Brother can you spare a
dime?

  —Words and music: Y. Harburg & Jay Gorney
  —Sung by Bing Crosby

The "great stock market crash" started in 1929 leading to a major depression that would continue and worsen till we entered World War II. It was not our first depression nor would it be our last. It revealed again those basic flaws in human nature and our capitalistic system; greed, over speculation and a lack of control by the government of our financial markets. In the late 1930's, just before entering the war, with a population of 123 million; 34 million had no way of earning a living. Two million men wandered the land from state to state and 15 million (25%) of our work force was idle. Many became desperate enough to start forest fires so that they could be hired to put them out and committed crimes in order to be jailed where at least they would be fed. Others sold apples for a nickel that they bought for 5 cents a box or went house to house looking for small jobs and hopefully a meal.

Like today, in spite of the high unemployment, the country did not shut down. New items such as radios and refrigerators became available and sold. People took up bowling, increased their attendance at baseball games and movies became better and more popular. Tourism actually increased with the introduction of better cars, roads and tourist cabins. It was an era of escape with Jazz, Comedies, Musicals and gangster movies. The country produced both Woody Guthrie and Rudy Vallee; the Rocket's and the Okies. We sang songs about better times to come:

> Blue skies, smiling at me, nothing but blue skies do I see.
> Blue birds, singing a song, nothing but bluebirds from now on.
> Never saw the sun shining so bright, never saw things going so right.
> Blue days, all of them gone, nothing but blue skies from now on.
> —Irving Berlin—ASCAP

OR

> Smile even though your heart is aching, smile even though it's breaking,
> When there are clouds in the sky you'll get by,
> If you smile through your fear and sorrow, smile and maybe tomorrow,
> You'll see the sun come shining through for you----
>
> —Charlie Chaplin, G. Parsons & J. Phillips ASCAP

We saw ourselves as a classless society where anyone could lift themselves up by their own bootstraps, just like my father always preached. How could it be possible with no jobs or opportunity that people would remain hopeful? It's not possible; a lack of jobs created unrest along with a resurgence in the communist party. In 1932 police fired on demonstrators at the Ford plant in Dearborn Michigan, killing four. During the summer of 1932 25,000 vets, members of the "Bonus Army", occupied Washington D.C. asking for the immediate implementation of the Adjusted Compensation Act for veterans. There was no sympathy for World War I vets who, unlike today, had received little compensation and were then driven out of Washington by our future hero; George Patton on orders from General McArthur. The unemployed crossed the country by box car looking for work. They built shanty towns along the tracks in large cities out of any discarded material they could find. In Seattle they built "Hooverville" near the rail yards on First Avenue South only to have the city tear it down and force the men to move on out of town. The politicians cared little where these men went as long as it was out of their city. It was a common solution in most cities and was driven by fear of possible crime. We still treat the disenfranchised the same; move them some place where the "good citizens" don't have to see them.

The country's poverty and misery was not ignored by the artists. Singer and composer, Woody Guthrie criss-crossed the country writing and singing songs about every problem that faced us including unemployement. John Steinbeck wrote "Grapes of Wrath" detailing the despair of farmers trying to escape the dust bowl. He was so poor himself that he did not have postage to mail in his manuscript. Yet, this era would produce Cole Porter, Bing Crosby, Cary Grant, F. Scott Fitzgerald and Lois Armstrong. The New Deal spawned the WPA that lasted for eight years and employed 11 million men. They, along with the CCC were responsible for many lasting works of art.

Both movies and radio helped Americans deal with the depression. The movies were part escapism and part social relevance. We laughed at movies like Topper, loved the musicals and yet related to Cagney the gangster who would not be pushed around or to King Kong and Frankenstein who only lashed out when hurt. We felt for the common man in the movies; George Bailey, Jefferson Smith or Longfellow Deeds. Gary Cooper's speech in "Met John Doe" is still poignant when he says:

> "I know a lot of you are saying, what can I do, I am just a little punk. I don't count. Well, you're dead wrong. The little punks have always counted, because in the long run the character of the country is the sum total of its little punks. But we all have to get in there and pitch."

I like to think there is just a chance this could still be true and that people could work together to solve the problems of wars, unemployment and the environment.

The radio was important during the depression and on thru the war. It did not require much money and a lot of people could gather around and listen at no cost. A daily program like Amos and Andy was so popular that the movies scheduled their times around it. The Radio not only served as entertainment, but was one of our main sources of news. As we grappled with our social issues we needed the escape offered by movies and radio.

12-42: Enrico Fermi produces the first nuclear chain reaction at the U. of Chicago.

1-43: Roosevelt and Churchill meet at Casablanca; Bergman has to leave, Bogart stays.

2-43: Germans surrender at Stalingrad and start to withdraw from Tunisia.

3-43: In four days German U-Boats sink 27 U.S. merchant ships.

4-43: Japan gives captured U.S. airmen "one way ticket to hell."

CHAPTER 6
THE OTHER BROTHER

You've got to ac-cent-tchu-ate the positive, E-limy-nate the negative-latch on to the affirmative, don't mess with mister in-between. You've got to spread joy up to the maximum, bring gloom down to the minimum, and have faith or pan-demonium liable to walk upon the scene.

M y brother, David Paine Thompson, nearly five years my sen-ior, had graduated from Garfield High School and was into his sophomore year of civil engineering at the University of Washington as I entered Garfield. I am sure my birth was an un-planned event and often regretted by my parents during the early years as I tended to be an unruly child. My parents would have been perfectly content with a single. Since there were no plans for a second child, Dave was given an extra supply of brains, leaving a shortage when I arrived five years later. He was the child parents dream of, but seldom get; tall, handsome, brainy and athletic. As if that were not enough he was a really nice person and well liked by all who knew him. I was glad to be five years behind as I entered Garfield, for it gave people time to forget him and not make comparisons.

David and I carried the same middle name of Paine. As mentioned earlier, genealogy was important to my mother and she made sure that

My Brother and Me 1943

we both had the name Paine somewhere so that we or our children would be eligible for organizations like the Daughters of the American Revolution and Sons of the Minute Men. Apparently it was not too important to either Dave or me, or any of our children as no one ever took advantage of those organizations open only to decedents of the Plymouth colony or of Minute Men. I think we both felt that since nearly everyone in America claims one of these early ancestors, what could be the big deal.

During his two years at the university he joined the Sigma Alpha Epsilon fraternity, turned out for crew and enlisted in the reserve or ROTC as it was called in college. On April 10th, 1941 he was called for active duty and sent to Camp Callan in California for basic training in anti-aircraft. Probably, due to his two years of college, he was then sent to Texas A&M to be trained for the Army Engineers. He was near San Diego long enough to enable mom and me to board the coastal train, visit her sister Lettie and see Dave on weekends. My mother had gone twice before to San Diego to visit her sister Lettie. The first time was with both David and I by tramp steamer when I was very young, maybe three or four years old. It was a memorable trip; first because we made our first stop after leaving Seattle at Washougal on the Columbia river where the sulfur smell of the pulp mill permeated everything and made me ill. Secondly, one day one of the crew men tried to frighten me by picking me up and holding me out over the ship rail, causing my mother to have a panic attack. David, on the other hand, had a great time practically living on the captain's bridge. Our second trip was just me and mother all the way by train to San Diego when I was a bit older and since the stay was longer I was enrolled in a nearby grade school. That stay became memorable when after school I went out a different door than I had entered becoming lost for several hours and causing my mother a second panic attack. Now, on this third trip, I was in high school, a teen and looking forward to being in warm, sunny San Diego with the extra freedom that comes with age.

It was nice for Dave to have his family nearby, for as was the case with most boys entering the service, he had never been away from home for an extended period except when he served as a group leader at Camp Meany, the Cub Scout camp on Hood Canal in Puget Sound. I had a much better time and did not have to worry about what lay ahead of me. My mother bought me an old bike and since San Diego was still a small town with little traffic, I was basically on my own. I divided my time between taking the trolley to the free and amazing San Diego zoo where I could ride their great carousel and try to reach for the gold ring off a galloping stead, or bike down town to catch a ferry to Coronado Island for body surfing in front of the Coronado Hotel. The only sign that there was a war were the miles of camouflage netting draped over the aircraft plants just as there was over Boeing on First South in Seattle. I guess I was too young and apathetic to feel guilty over having such a great time. So, what's the difference between ignorance and apathy? I don't know and I don't care!

On June 6th, 1944 the Allied forces mounted a counter offensive, landing troops at Normandy Beach on the northern coast of France. The fighting was fierce and bloody with immense casualties on both sides. More bodies were quickly needed to make up for our losses. David and others in engineering in Texas were taken out of school, given short training on the use of the heavy BAR gun and hurriedly shipped off to France. They were ill prepared for what was to come. He arrived in France late in the winter of 1944 and sent straight to the front. He and his regiment arrived at the front just in time to be greeted by a massive German counter offensive through the wooded Ardennes region of South Belgium on December 16, 1944. The Allied forces were caught by surprise and my brother along with hundreds of others was captured on his first day in battle. Not good but better than several alternatives.

We stopped hearing from him, feared for the worst, but kept our hopes up as hearing nothing is often best. As it turned out, he was sent to one of the Stalag camps where he was put to work in a steel mill. He was strong and athletic, probably weighing 215 pounds at the time of his capture and more than capable of doing hard work; just what the Germans wanted as they had run short of male workers. Besides running short of labor, the Germans were also running short of food, so that the prisoners would only receive a watery bowl of potato or beet soup a day. He and others were slowly starving and getting weaker as his weight dropped by 100 pounds. On days when they did not work at the mill they would be sent out to the surrounding farms to help harvest sugar beets, some of which, being famished, they ate. Too many beets gave Dave dysentery and on one trip back from the farm he passed out. The guards would have left him, but two of his prison mates carried him back to camp where he was placed on a cot and left for dead. To everyone's amazement the following day he awoke and with the help of a British doctor in the camp he was nursed back to a semblance of health. On April 17th, 1945 he was freed by our advancing troops.

I was home alone when we received notice that he was alive. I withheld the notice for one day and presented it to my father that night to celebrate his birthday. The best gift he would ever receive.

Dave returned home on a troop ship, but unfortunately was allowed to over eat too soon for a person in his condition, resulting in yellow jaundice and a huge distended stomach. After a long stay in an Army hospital he was able to regain his strength, return to college and even captain the varsity crew for several years. He would not marry the girl he had gone with before entering the service. This came as a shock to me as she lived nearby in Montlake and we related well with each other. Instead, another girl named Barbara Cushing, had taken up writing to Dave while he was away, probably because both parents were friends and they knew servicemen liked to receive mail no matter who sends it. She had written him faithfully and Dave must have liked what she said for shortly after returning home the two were married; Dave returning to study civil engineering and Barbara working as an early courtroom recorder. Dave was a whiz at math and engineering and would graduate with top honors. In later years I sought him out to assist me through calculus, but to no avail, even with his tutoring it failed to stick in my brain and I was forced to drop out of engineering.

So Dave never returned to live with us, nor would he spend time at our summer cabin on Vashon Island as I would continue doing. Upon graduation he accepted a position with Standard Oil of California where he remained for a number of years and was instrumental in developing off shore drilling in the Gulf of Mexico. This was an accomplishment he may have felt differently about had he still been alive when hurricanes Katrina and Rita slammed into the Gulf coast in 2005 destroying 108 oil structures and causing 7.1 million gallons of oil to spill into gulf waters, or theBritish Petroleum spill in 2010. David's father in law was president of Citizens Federal Savings and Loan in down town Seattle. Like me, he knew Dave was exceptionally smart and so convinced him to come to work for the bank. This started Dave's second career and would lead eventually to him becoming bank president.

His father in law was an avid boater and owned a unique craft that had originally been built for Hermann Goering, head of the German Luftwaffe. How it came to be in Seattle was a mystery. My parents and I spent many good days on this hand crafted yacht watching Dave in crew races or Stan Sayres great hydroplane, Slomo IV race against the Pepsi or the fateful Quick Silver. Dave would follow in Mr. Cushing's footsteps and become a skipper, mooring the boat in the front yard of his Meydenbauer home near Kirkland.

What ever David did he did it well. He made friends easily and kept them all his life. Many of his friends he traced back to Montlake and high school. He was not only my brother, but my best friend. He would not live the long life of either of his parents and developed liver cancer probably as a consequence of his stint in the prison camp. He died at age 79, but while alive he lived life to the fullest.

5-43: Japanese withdraw from the Aleutian Is.

7-43 Allied troops land in Sicily & Italy surrenders; German fights on in Italy.

8-43: John Kennedy's P.T. boat sunk.

11-43: Stalin, Roosevelt & Churchill meet in Teheran, Iran. (during better times) Churchill states, "Americans will always do the right thing after all other options are exhausted."

1943: Frank Sinatra's first concert in New York with Tommy Dorsey. 30,000 bobby soxers riot.

1944: U.S. & Britain regain Gilbert Is., Solomons, Marianas, Burma & New Guinea.

CHAPTER 7
THE POISON PILL OF WARS

No tears, no fears, remember, there's always tomorrow, so what if we have to part, we'll be together again. Your kiss, your smile, are memories I'll treasure forever, so try thinking with your heart, we'll be together again.

—C. Fisher & Frankie Laine ASCAP

It's like in the movie "Ground Hog Day", we fight one war and wake up 20 years later and were fighting that same war again; then comes Korea, then Vietnam, Iraq and Afghanistan. Will we ever wake up? World War I had morphed into World War II largely due to the failure of the United States congress to ratify the treaty of Versailles, thus weakening the United Nations, which in turn was unable to prevent Japan's expansion into Manchuria and China; Italy's conquest of Ethiopia and Germany's seizure of Austria.

War seldom solves the problem for which it was originally fought; that usually being to add territory, to get at another countries raw materials or ethnic cleansing of a people they feel are their inferiors or believe in the wrong God. Countries always have moral reasoning for going to war and all countries are certain God is on their side. In past history, the Jews' exterminated the Canaanites because the Jews coveted their land

and the Canaanites worshipped a God other than Jehovah. The Nazis appropriation of Slavic land was to them moral because the Slavs were considered an inferior race. Mass murder of Jews was again viewed as moral to prevent pollution of the German race. In the 1930's in Germany one in two marriages were mixed causing, as Hitler said, "a dilution of the Arian race." In the Bush era the torture of prisoners at Abu-Grab and Guantanamo was viewed as moral because "our" God hates terrorists and so they do not merit humane protection.

In Russia, World War I turned into a civil war led by Lenin and the Bolshevists in an effort to terminate the unjust rule of the Czars. This brought to power Stalin who was much more ruthless than the Czars, imprisoning 20 million dissidents, establishing brutal Gulag prison camps and pioneering ethnic cleansing on the reasoning that a multinational empire was unreliable. The first modern day genocide was when Turkey killed 1.5 million Armenians and expelled all Greeks from Anatolia. The Armenians never have and never will forget this.

As the Allies waged their "just war" in the 1940's it soon became a war between evil and lesser evil. We and our Allies gradually adopted techniques that we had at one time criticized the enemy for using. Unfortunately, as wars progress both sides try to de-humanize each other. We treat each other worse than animals making everyone want to "fight to the death". The battles then become more brutal and racial. I remember making large posters in junior high and used wording that made the Japanese and Germans seem less than human. As the chance for a Japanese or German victory ebbed and we insisted on unconditional surrender, the intensity of the war increased and the Allies stepped up their war against the civilian population; the very policy we had earlier criticized. America heavily bombed Tokyo, destroyed Dresden and decimated Hiroshima and Nagasaki; forever regretting that we were the ones that issued in the atomic age. We always claimed our actions were justified for we were fighting evil. The destructive machines we invent are always a step ahead of our morals.

The "God is on our side" philosophy is the most used reason to justify human conflicts as seen in World War I and II, in the Bush invasion of Iraq and in the dispute between Israel and Hamas over the Gaza Strip. These are examples of noble justification for unwarranted invasion. Religions often form a simplistic façade that veils knowledge and so forms a barrier to understanding. Humans, being complicated and contrary creatures, tend to cling to their comfortable beliefs to the last man standing.

World War II may have been the last "industrial conflict" where massive armies slug it out on the field of battle. We now fight for political advantage and public opinion as much as for victories which are increasingly harder to come by due to the gorilla nature of war. European countries came to this realization sooner than the U.S and withdrew from most of their colonies after WW II, not from defeat, but from the realization that they were no longer able to secure their political objectives. Freedom from foreign occupation has become the political ideal of our times. America, disregarding it's often voiced commitment to human freedom, replaced Britain in Iran, Iraq and Saudi Arabia; France in Vietnam and Russia in Afghanistan. All are similarly doomed to failure with the rise in anti colonialism throughout the world.

1-44: Soviets re-occupy Poland; Allies heavily bomb German industries.

1-44: Allies enter Rome; D Day landing at Normandy. (Private Ryan saved) First V1 rocket hits Britain.

7-44: Attempt made to assassinate Hitler by his own men fails.

8-44: Soviets Occupy Hungary & Estonia. Civil war starts in Greece.

8-14-44: African American soldiers riot at Fort Lawton, Seattle and lynch an Italian prisoner of war, claiming unfair treatment of blacks.

CHAPTER 8
DING DONG; THE BELLS

Missed the Saturday dance, heard they crowded the floor, couldn't bear it without you, don't get around much any-more. Thought I'd visit the club, I got as far as the door, They'd have asked me about you, Don't get around much anymore.

—Duke Ellington & Bob Russell 1942 ASCAP

Our neighbors, from age six till graduation from Garfield, were the Bells. We remained, they eventually moved on. There were three children; two boys, Bob and Remi and a daughter Helen. Remi, a year my senior, and I spent a lot of time together especially when younger. Mr. Bell answered to the name of "Ding" when called by his wife, Florence. He was slight of build, rather soft spoken and came across as one who came from a moneyed upbringing as he was a Harvard graduate and an avid tennis player. The family arrived in Seattle at the height of the depression and like many he was unemployed.

Mrs. Bell, on the other hand, was full bodied and often reminded me of the diva Kate Smith. There was little question as to whom was the boss of this household and she could be extremely haughty when chal-lenged. A branch of Mrs. Bell's family owned two of the larger laundries in Seattle and lived in what I likened to be a mansion at the top of Capi-tol Hill. Remi and I would visit them at times and play miniature golf on the third floor links and listen to weird records played on a huge wind up victrola. Being young and impressionable, this seemed to construe wealth. They also owned the less successful Sunshine Laundry near Green Lake which was turned over or sold to the Bells.

Mrs. Bell may have come on a little strong, but she was one hard worker and if you were around her for a while it would not be long before she had you also working. When they took over the laundry it came with one old black chevy panel truck with "Sunshine Laundry" painted on the side. It made the deliveries, took "Ding" back and forth to work and on Sundays took the family to church at St. Johns on Capitol Hill; come hell or high water. This was a work truck and had only one seat for the driver, so Mrs. Bell would place a box in front to sit on and the kids would crawl in and out the back door, sitting on the floor. To Florence, Catholicism was serious business and she made sure the children and Ding were well indoctrinated. Remi missed many neighborhood events because of either Saturday catechism or church. We were in the same Cub Scout and Boy Scout troops and I recall one overnight campout and hike to Cougar Mountain near Issaquah. The area was still fairly wild and remote and to get there we had to drive around the south end of Lake Washington through Renton as there was not yet a floating bridge. We're all up lighting fires and fixing breakfast on Sunday morning and Remi starts insisting the Scoutmaster take him into the nearest church before a lightning bolt strikes him down. Talk about the fear of God!

Remi was talented and inventive as a boy and an adult. When radios were hard to find he built a crystal set that brought in our few stations. He taught himself to play the trumpet and the piano which he still plays. When he became eligible to drive he also worked on engines for race cars and re-built an old Indian motorcycle. After graduating college he put his creative abilities to work, first for the small United Controls and his remaining years with Boeing.

The Bell's hard work started to pay off and the laundry became so successful they were able to move, building a new home in the desirable district of Laurelhurst; at least right on the very edge. Mrs. Bell had located an empty lot just where one enters Laurelhurst. It also fronted on a marshy area that connected to the Montlake ship canal. I am sure it had been ignored by others as being too wet and soggy to build on, but she saw the potential and built a beautiful home on the high ground and a large lawn on fill sloping down to a bulkhead. There was a little water front and a narrow opening out to the main channel; it must be time to go boating. Under Mrs. Bell's supervision much of the work was done by the family and any of Remi's friend's who wandered by.

Remi's friend, Stan Wright, had bought an almost finished hull of a plywood speedboat but it was still in need of an engine. Whom do you turn to? Of course, Remi the "engine man". On Evergreen Point in Bellevue, Stan Sayres, an auto dealer, had been an avid limited boat racer, but was now in the process of building his first unlimited hydroplane. He thus had a surplus six cylinder Lycoming airplane engine used in his limited hydro's which Remi was able to purchase and install in Stan's boat. The boat was light and bare bones, the engine was powerful and the boat went very, very fast. The purpose behind all this was so that we could learn the new sport of water skiing. The problem was that we only were aware of two or three people that knew how to water ski and no one that sold skis. Remi turned to Wally Burr who built snow skis, and Wally agreed to try his hand at his first pair of water skis.

It just happened that at this same time the University was remodeling the old shell house on the Montlake Ship Ccanal and had "surplused" several of their large sliding doors and left them floating nearby. Remi borrowed one and towed it back where it became our dock and a starting platform for skiing. Perfect, just sit on the edge, skis in the water and be jerked out through the narrow opening into open water. The bay was the perfect place to learn to ski; out of the wind and with very slow boat traffic. In 1926, Don Ibsen, a senior at Roosevelt High School had screwed a pair of tennis shoes on to some cedar boards, thus becoming the co-inventor of a sport that would sweep the world. (The other man was from Minnesota)

Haste to get the boat in the water so that we could ski resulted in putting off a few of the finishing details. First, the gear shift was at the very back of the engine so that if alone in the boat you would first start the engine in neutral, go to the back, put it in gear and quickly go back up front to accelerate and steer. Second, steering was just by light ropes which we always intended to change to braided wire. The inevitable happened, one day while in the little cove at Remi's someone got in a hurry and started the engine while still in gear and with the throttle advanced. The boat was pointed right at the float and accelerated jumping out of the water, across the shell house door and ending up twenty feet on to the neighbor's lawn, leaving the prop and drive shaft stuck in the float. We never did correct that problem, but did become more careful.

There was one other incident that did really scare me. On one sunny day we were out jetting around with me at the wheel. I spied some friends lounging on the stern of the Spirit, a fifty foot sailboat owned by the Augustine's. Deciding to be a smart ass I buzzed the boat at full speed, making a sharp turn to the left just short of the side and thus throwing up a huge spray of water over everyone on board. I sped on a hundred feet, went to make a right turn and to my horror found the steering cable had parted. How close is that to disaster? Is there someone looking after me or what? Over two summers we learned to water ski, but Stan, the boat's owner, neither swam or water skied, but did let us use his boat whenever we needed to ski. Since we used it much more than Stan, he finally sold it and purchased a Star class sailboat; he needed a crew, I volunteered. That became the start of many years racing sailboats.

By 1954 Remi and I had both avoided the draft by remaining in college. We received our draft notice at the same time, had our physicals and got our induction notices. The war was over, but the draft continued for there was no Blackwater mercenaries and we still needed occupation troops. It was time for an "induction party" at Remi's house which was held a few days before we left. It was men only except for two strippers. Great party right up to the end when there was a slight misunderstanding about how much to pay one of the girls. She felt we cheated her, got really, really mad, rushed out of the house, jumped in her car and proceeded to ram several of our autos that were parked in front. This created a great deal of excitement especially when the neighbors and police showed. It turned an ordinary stag event into a very memorable party. We went for induction and Remi left, but as my vision was below standard without my glasses, I was given the choice of going in the Army or home. That was a tough decision, you guess.

6-44: U.S. bombs Japanese factories in Thailand.

6-44: Germans counter attack at Ardennes. (David is captured)Gen. Patton lands in Fr.

9-44: Soviets occupy Hungary and Estonia.

10-44: First Kamikaze attack on U.S. ships. 2,257 attacks by end of war.

CHAPTER 9
THOSE EARLY GIRLS

I'm in the mood for love, simply because your near me,
Funny, but when your near me, I'm in the mood for love.
Heaven is in your eyes, bright as the stars we're under, Oh,
is it any wonder, I'm in the mood for love?

—Jimmy McHugh & Dorothy Fields ASCAP

My father taught me to appreciate the intricacies of baseball by driving me south on 23rd Avenue to Sick's stadium to watch the then Seattle Rainer's play ball. It was a small, intimate ball park with a hill rising from left field where kids and adults with good vision could watch for free. Living close, we went often when the team was in town, always sitting in the right field bleachers where dad felt we had the best chance of catching a foul ball. He taught me that an important part of watching a ball game was to verbally harass the opposing players, at which I became quite good. Many of the players such as Bill Laurence, Fred Hutchison, Edo Vanie and Dick Barrett played for the Rainer's over many years and thus extracted a loyal following. The play was broadcast by Leo Lassen and it was only after I was older that I learned he was not really present at our out of town games, but only adlibbed the plays from a direct telephone line. I was always fairly good at baseball, probably due to the time dad and I spent playing catch in front of our house. I did start to turn out while in high school, but the old problem of staying late for practice reared its head. My father also taught me the importance of mowing, watering and weeding our small lawn, for which I would receive a small pittance called "my allowance".

Those really important things, like manners, and how to hold a knife and fork I learned from my mother. She was not strict, but did believe in proper conduct and could be quite repetitive till finally she achieved the necessary behavior. She strongly felt that no adult or child should utter a swear word or take the name of the Lord in vain. It's lucky she never lived long enough to see Chris Rock on Television. Children could talk, but should never butt in when an adult was talking. When eating, no elbows on the table, chew with the mouth shut (still working on that), put your napkin in the lap and do not start eating till the last person is served (hard to do with 16 people at Thanksgiving dinner). To leave the dinner table after eating, ask to be excused. By eating out at a semi formal restaurant once a week, plus dressing up, I was infused with manners at an early age making my behavior charming, but quickly forgotten as I aged. Quite a contrast to the free for all that exists at most dinner tables today.

She felt boys should know how to dance if they ever wish to be around girls. I was just at that age when I was not really sure if I wanted to be around them or not. On those rainy days Mr. Hagger, our P.E. teacher had us doing the Shottish in the girl's gym at Montlake elementary. I preferred it when we played dodge ball, but if I had to get close to a girl I wanted it to be Gloria to whom I felt some attraction. While still in grade school Gloria and I were invited to my first (and last) girl-boy party at Glo's house. This was also my introduction to spin the bottle. The winner (or looser depending) did not have to remove any clothing, but instead went into the closet with a girl on the assumption they would kiss. I was not ready to go that far with a girl at such a tender age, so I just acted like an idiot; very easy to do at that early age.

The experience was not completely bad and I definitely felt there was something to the boy-girl relation; an attraction I had not previously experienced. Unusual things were also going on in my genital region that I could not control. I would often awake in the morning and find my pajamas wet and it was not from urine. When I would shinny up a rope or a pole it felt strangely good, then better and better till finally peaking, leaving me a little weak. I was having a hard time leaving the poles alone just like Woody Allen and his "Orb" in the movie, "Sleeper". If my mother knew about masturbation or wet dreams, she did not care to share her knowledge with me. Of course she was raised in a home full of girls and probably was not too sure herself what was going on. Neither was there any information coming from the schools. Whatever it was I would have to figure it out on my own. Luckily I only became nearsighted and did not go blind.

One day I invited my neighbor Evelyn into the basement to show her a model airplane that I was building. At least I felt that was my motive, but suddenly I grabbed and kissed her, much to hers and my surprise. She rushed home to tell her parents who told my parents who then gave me my first talk on birds and bees which was not my parent's best subject. If I had been more knowledgeable I would have told them it was just a kiss, not a rape. Parents today would be relieved to know that their son had kissed the neighbor's daughter and not the neighbor's son.

One other neighbor was JoAnne who lived on the next street and was just old enough do a little babysitting. Remi Bell, Joe Damski and I would sometimes show up after the parents left in the hope of stealing a kiss. She was a beautiful girl even at this young age and remained a knockout all her life. Apparently she did not find me as attractive as I found her for I was never lucky. Joe made out better and the two went out together for a time.

At my mother's insistence I soon found myself in a weekly dance class held somewhere in the re-grade district. She chauffeured me and to my embarrassment sometimes waited and watched till the class was over. There is nothing like having your mother around while you're trying to be cool with the girls. I overcame my nervousness with humor and being the class cut-up. It worked well then and it worked for many years after. I liked music, always could hold a tune and found that the rhythm and movements in dancing came naturally. We were taught the basics; Fox Trot, Samba, Tango and Waltz all of which came in handy in the future. We learned to properly ask a girl to dance, how to hold, lead and avoid stepping on her feet. I like what George Elliot said- "Life seems to go on without effort when I am filled with music." Most important though, this was where I would meet my first real girl friend, Lilly Jean.

Lilly Jean - My first girl friend

My mother found out that Lilly lived only three blocks from our home in Montlake and had to come to class and return home by bus; something unheard of today. In 1940 if the family had a car the husband usually drove it to work. When my mother learned of this, Lilly was soon riding with us and in a natural progression I was soon seeing Lilly after school and in the evening. I was still getting around on a bike so we stayed close to her home, spending a lot of time on the living room couch. Her mother left us alone just enough so that we could practice kissing and exploratory stuff. My approach was to learn by doing. Our kissing, on a scale of ten, was about a two as I had little knowledge of a girl's anatomy having grown up without a sister and in a home where I only saw my mother when she was in full attire. I, like most children, can never picture their parents having sex and are more than willing to believe the stork story.

At this age it was a mystery as to what girls expected from boys and I remain a little confused to this day. We probably both wanted the same thing, but were not sure of the proper approach. Sex or "health" education was not taught in high school till our senior year. The class was male only and very hush, hush; the only advice I remember receiving was "keep it in your pants" and "don't come inside a girl"; advice that a parent could hardly improve upon even today. His center point I am sure was abstinence as I cannot recall any mention of a prophylactic. I was not really aware of what some called "rubbers", but there was a raw sewerage outlet at the foot of Hamlin Street next to the Seattle Yacht club and mixed in with the excrement were these long white objects. My friends and I speculated as to their use, but settled on balloons.

Lilly Jean and I had a mutually exploratory relationship that lasted off and on for many years, but remained more friendship than lover. I imagine all teenagers, especially boys, go through an awkward stage when first dating. With me, it took a relationship with an "older girl" to teach me the art of kissing. Not being able to drive made it doubly awkward to go on a date as we either had to ride the bus or go through the embarrassment of having my parents drive us both ways. This I only did two times, both with Doris, the only girl I would date from Garfield. The first date was to a movie with two or three other couples from school. A nice date and everything went well. On second date Doris asked me to a dance at the Women's University Club in down town Seattle. It was a dance where the girls wore party dresses and the boys wore dark suits. This was my introduction to that "middle world" that lies between adolescence and adulthood; a time, especially for boys, where they learn not to act quite so stupid in public and around girls. Besides that, they get to practice wearing adult clothes. It's the sort of event promoted by adults in the hope that boys will start acting like little gentlemen and stop embarrassing their parents.

The party could have turned out really great, as I had been doing well with my dance lessons and had the basic moves down fairly well, however I did not own a dark suit and my parents were not convinced that the occasion warranted buying one. I attended the dance as the only boy wearing a tan sport coat with dark brown slacks. How embarrassing was that? It's amazing the small events that remain locked in a person's mind forever. I do not feel this was a determining factor, but I would not go out with any other girl from Garfield.

Seattle is a great place during the summer. No matter what district you live in one is never far from parks and water. My home was half a block from the center of the University of Washington Arboretum. I could cut through a neighbor's yard and in seconds be in the woods, or hop on my bike, taking the trail past the Broadmoor driving range and in ten minutes be at the "point" where Lake Washington joined the ship canal. We either swam at the point or at the entrance to the Montlake cut, directly across from the University of Washington Shell House where they stored both rowing shells and rental canoes. What we called the "cut" was simply the short deep channel that connected the lake to Portage Bay and was spanned by the Montlake Bridge leading to the university campus. In digging the cut they had left a rather steep cliff on the Montlake side that gradually rose higher until it was about 20 to 25 feet high. If a swimmer took a running leap off the high ground he could just clear the underwater shelf that jutted out five to ten feet from the base of the cliff before dropping off sharply into deep water. A little scary on that first jump, but it's the type of risks teenagers relish taking; after all we are going to live forever.

Madison Beach at the foot of Madison Street was our closest public beach and from Montlake it required peddling up and down a couple hills. The big attraction was that it was directly adjacent to the terminal for the Kirkland ferry. Two small ferries still ran on Lake Washington, the other went from Leschi to Mercer Island. Both were stopped after the floating bridge was finished in 1941. When the ferry came in to dock at Madison we would swim in under the loading ramp and catch the backwash from the front propeller as it was used to slow the ferry for docking. The strong current produced would flush us out from under the dock for twenty or thirty feet. This was repeated when the ferry again left to return to Kirkland. This brought on a lot of shouting from the Captain and crew about the danger involved. As if that was not irritating the Captain enough we would occasionally climb up a piling and onto the upper ferry deck just as it was pulling out and the crew were busy with lines. We would ride the ferry out twenty feet, dive off as a crewman was about to grab us and swim back to shore. The good Captain always had a few choice words of advice for us swimmers.

I found that I was going more and more to the "point" as this was where girls often came to swim as opposed to jumping off the ferry or a cliff into the canal. It was on one of those great summer days swimming at the point that I met my second girl friend, Betty. She was cute, dark haired and Irish, but she lived at the top of Capital Hill in one of those large old homes built close to her catholic church and school; Holly Names. I walked her to the bus stop and was able to muster enough courage to obtain her phone number and start a new relationship. Going out with a Catholic girl did not sit well with my mother who was a firm believer in the separation of the Church of England from the Papacy. I tried to explain that it was only a date not an engagement. As Chris Rock said, "A man is basically as faithful as his options." Goodbye Lilly Jean.

De-ja-vu, going with Betty was a lot like going with Lilly Jean except that instead of riding my bike a few blocks I now had to hop a bus to the top of Capital Hill and walk another five blocks to Betty's home on 18th. I was still necking and feeling around but with a new girl and on a new couch. Then, on a Friday during the school year my friend George talked me into going to a teen dance he had heard about instead of going on my regular date with Betty. This dance was held every Friday in the Wilsonian Hotels' ballroom and was sponsored by Margret Tapping who held dance classes in the same room during the week. George had heard that a lot of girls attended and he was correct. I had somehow neglected to call Betty who did not take kindly to being stood up and resulted in my not seeing her again, but in exchange a new world of dance opened up.

The dance was held on the ground floor ballroom with an admission of 25 cents. Music was by everyone's favorite vocalists and big bands via nickelodeon. The place was packed with teens doing a dance my instructor failed to teach. It fascinated both George and me, but with no experience all we could do was just watch. There is nothing worse for a boy than being turned down when he asks a girl to dance other than being accepted and then not knowing how to dance. Our early approach was to only look and learn.

We tried to absorb what the dancers were doing so maybe we could practice before we attended another dance. The couples moved always in a counter clock direction and remained pressed together. The majority of the time the boy faced forward and seemed to be pushing the girl as she moved backward. They took long sliding steps made possible by wax that was occasionally sprinkled on the floor making it quite slippery. It seemed leather shoe were a necessity as this allowed the dancers to slide at the end of each step. Every once in a while the couples would make this graceful turn and the boy would move backwards for a few steps and then smoothly turn again and go forward. They danced mainly to slow music sung by Sinatra, Jo Stafford, Helen O'Connell or the Ink Spots. Once or twice during the night they played a fast song that two or three couples could Jitterbug to, while everyone else watched. No one wore Nikes or hiking boots, there were no weird gyrations or flailing of arms and the dancers remained together instead of being two feet apart each doing their own dance. We were fascinated and knew this was the dance we wanted to learn. We watched, absorbed the movements and then went home to practice the best we could with only each other as partners. We attended more dances and would finally summon up the courage to ask girls to dance. We finally did start to learn this new dance that was called the Avalon. At first we asked girls that seemed to be beginners like us, but we gradually became more confident as our dancing improved. Through the years we would attend stag dances in all parts of the city and at many lakes around Seattle that had small dance halls. Dancing the Avalon would become an addiction.

10-44: U.S. bombs Okinawa, Truk and Tokyo again.

12-44: U.S. invades Philippines & retakes most of islands.

12-44: Gen. Patton's troops help stall Germans at the bulge.

CHAPTER 10
SURVIVING THE WAR

Dream when your feel-in' blue, Dream that's the thing to do,
Just watch the smoke rings rise in the air, you'll find your
share of memories there so dream when the day is through,
dream and they may come true.

—Johnny Mercer—1944

The Japanese felt that their attacks on Pearl Harbor and the Philippine Islands would cripple us in the Pacific. Instead, the sneakiness of their attack just pissed off the whole country. I do not think that our country has ever been so unified before or since that attack. It seemed like our production lines changed overnight from consumer goods to military hardware. Up to the start of the war the country was still bogged down in a depression. At our home in Montlake men came by regularly looking to do work for food. They never begged, but were always willing to do anything for a meal. We really had no work, but my mother never let a man leave our house without a bag of sandwiches. Unlike today, even with desperate men going house to house, we never feared for our safety. During the depression years and on through high school I do not remember anything being taken from anyone's yard or car. The front door of our home was never locked and it was not till I was out of high school that I started to carry a key to the front door.

As Descartes said, "everyone experiences life from their own point of view." I remember on one occasion a man came to the door looking for work. My mother told him there was no work, but for him to wait while she fixed him a few sandwiches. While he was on our porch I made some smart ass comment about him being a tramp. He was a proud man and I deeply hurt his feelings for he immediately took off walking up the street. When mother came with the sandwiches I had to explain why he was gone. She told me to take those sandwiches and go after him. I took them and ran after the man trying to apologize, but I had offended him too deeply for him to now accept. I felt so small and sad. This incident must have left a lasting impression on me, for since that time I seldom ignore a needy person on the street asking for help. I do not judge them. I am a believer in the six degrees of separation; I just happened to be the luckier one at that moment.

During the early part of the depression Roosevelt had instituted stock market and bank reforms along with public works projects using the government paid WPA and CCC work forces. There were many skilled workers and artisans among these two groups and it would not be till after the war that we fully realized the amazing accomplishments of these two groups. Our great national parks are a result of their talents and labors. As we geared for war, these skilled people would be absorbed into the work force and there would be no further great lodges built in our national parks. As I write this my country is once again facing a devastating depression brought on by long years of trying to police the world, first against communism and now against terrorists. We no longer fight hand to hand battles; we are not even sure where the enemy is hiding. A small band of terrorists have been able to bring this country and much of the world to its knees. It seems the longer we remain in foreign countries the stronger the opposition grows. Maybe we need public projects once again to restart the economy and rebuild the country's infrastructure.

After December 7th, 1941 the adjustment to a war time economy seemed to occur overnight. Car maker's changed to tanks and jeeps, Boeing made the Flying Fortress, Todd and Kaiser Shipyards replaced ships sunk by German U Boats and the naval shipyard in Bremerton repaired damaged naval vessels. Newport News ship yards on the east coast turned out submarines. In record time the country replaced what had been lost at Pearl Harbor plus much more. The dust bowl had led to many people migrating to the west coast. Now the country experienced a much larger population shift as people moved to where they were needed for the war industries. In the northwest they flooded into Seattle and Portland changing forever the demographics of both cities. With so many men entering the armed services women were being put to work doing what men had once done. Whether this was good or bad can still be debated, but women would never again be satisfied to remain at home being the house wife. When industries in the northwest looked for needed workers they found a large supply of Blacks in the south. Since at the start of the war most heavy industry was in the north, both the south and Midwest were heavily recruited. Both Blacks and Whites were brought in by the train load. Incoming Blacks settled first around 23rd and East Madison where there had been a small group for many years. As the area became saturated they moved south along 23rd avenue and along Rainer Avenue. During the war most of the Black teenagers attended my high school, Garfield. In my 1946 graduation class of 192 seniors there were only 12 that were Black. By the time I had my children Blacks would become a majority and White students would be bused in to Garfield to achieve a racial balance.

In March of 1942 the government quietly rounded up 120,000 American citizens of Japanese decent along the Pacific coast and shipped them inland to desolate concentration camps in Idaho and California. President Roosevelt's executive order #9066 authorized the secretary of war to designate military zones from which "any or all persons" may be excluded. In spite of this order 17,000 Japanese American citizens would sign up to fight for the United States. They would distinguish themselves in battle, but were not mixed with Caucasians.

One Japanese American, Minoru Yasui, decided he would test the constitutionality of the President's order. He was born in Hood River, Oregon where his parents were fruit growers. He obtained a law degree from the University of Oregon in 1939 where he was a member of the ROTC and later received his commission as a second lieutenant in the

Army's infantry reserve. Being Japanese he found it hard to find work in Portland so went east to Chicago. A week after Pearl Harbor, being a loyal American, he returned to Oregon to report for active duty, but was denied on nine separate occasions. Instead he was arrested by the F.B.I. as an enemy alien and had his assets frozen. On March 28, 1942 he deliberately broke the military curfew in Portland to test the law and later defied an executive order to evacuate and instead visited his parents in Hood River. At his trial on November 16, 1942 the judge stated that it was unconstitutional to apply curfew laws to citizens, but he felt Yasui had demonstrated loyalty to Japan so could no longer be considered a U.S. citizen. The case went all the way to the Supreme Court where Yasui was defended by the ACLU. On June 21, 1943 the court did find that the government had the authority to restrict the lives of civilians during war time. President Bush later used the same ruling to inter American citizens at Guantanamo during our invasion of Iraq. Fear rather than logic often motivates our decisions during times of war. Recently, to ease their guilt, the University of California at Los Angeles gave honorary degrees to all Japanese Americans who were interred during WWII while attending that school.

Seattle's racial changes during the war were more apparent at Garfield than at other city high schools. Since most of the city's Black population prior to 1941 had been centered around 23rd and Madison, the new arrivals also settled here. As the area became saturated they spread south and very slowly into what had been all white districts. As I entered High School the Japanese would be sent east to Moses Lake, Washington and Hunt, Idaho where they stayed for the war. After the war a few returned to Seattle and eight children re-enrolled at Garfield becoming part of my graduation class. Unfortunately by this time their parents had lost most of their possessions and property.

The nature of the Japanese attack at Pearl caused an immense amount of hatred and anger that was directed toward the Japanese at the start of the war. This was often physical and many felt the government had moved Japanese families inland for their own protection. Most in the Chinese community wore yellow badges to denote they were not Japanese. I am not sure if the government sponsored a hate campaign against the Japanese, but I remember in Junior High art class making posters that said mean things about the Japanese as a race. I guess this is normal during wars as each country tries to demean the people they fight making it easier to kill them.

We may not have posted signs like in the south, but there was a lot of spoken and unspoken discrimination in all the northwest; not all of it was directed toward the Japanese. At the start of the war there were no Black teachers in Seattle public schools. Blacks did not go to the public beaches except occasionally to Madrona. Most restaurants refused service to non-whites. A popular restaurant in both Seattle and Portland was the Coon Chicken Inn to which my parents often went. We never considered the inference of the name. Around 150,000 men migrated to the Seattle area; 25,000 of those were Black and about half returned home after the war. Discrimination was even worse in Oregon which had an active Ku Klux Klan. Real estate agents would not show homes to non-white, as a result the government had to build special housing around the city to house the new arrivals. In Portland they built the Vanport community that housed about 12,000 workers and were one of the very early integrated communities. Unfortunately they built it below the level of the Columbia River, protected only by a railroad dike. In 1948 the dike ruptured wiping out the entire community.

This flood of minorities that arrived in Seattle were shut out of unions so could not become boilermakers, plumbers or electricians thus leading to high unemployment after the war when retaining your job might be dependent on union membership. They instead became janitors, domestics, waiters and red caps. It was not till a while after the war's end that schools and the Post Office became the first to start hiring a few Blacks.

The prejudices built into our society over generations would be slow to disappear. Working and fighting for a common cause helped bring people together that previously had little interracial contact. The prejudice extended into the armed services where Blacks were not allowed to carry guns or fight In the front lines as we did not want them to be seen killing whites even though they were Germans or Japanese. Think of the movie Pearl Harbor where Cuba Gooding comes up from the kitchen to man an antiaircraft gun. Slowly the barriers have been broken down and most Seattle districts have been integrated. I am sorry to say that my parents moved to Magnolia because Montlake was becoming too mixed, but they did sell to a black family.

World War II would be our last "necessary" war and the last war where the country would be united and mobilized. I do not believe there was an adult or child whom did not contribute in some way to the war effort. In contrast to today, all men were treated equal and were required to register for the draft regardless of age or social status. We each received a classification depending on age, the type of work you were doing, if you were the only bread winner or if you were in school. As they initiated the draft in 1940 the first selected were drawn from a fish bowl to show the draft was un-biased. Further selections were made by local draft boards set up all across the country. The draft selections were made by our neighbors, usually those too old to serve. A war fought on two fronts needs a lot of bodies so there were few reasons for deferment; too young, too old, medical problem or you have a strategic job. This was democracy in action; a welling up of patriotism with lines at recruitment centers. Our present war in Iraq is fought by some regular Army, some reticent reservist and 150,000 hired mercenaries. A few like Pat Tillman felt a patriotic calling and left a lucrative pro football career to enlist in the Army, but look what it got him. Even though the government lied to get us involved in the Iraq war there were not a lot of objections. As Shakespeare said in Henry VI on the fickleness of the crowd:

> Look, As I blow this feather from my face, and as the air blows it to me again, obeying with my wind when I do blow, and yielding to another when it blows, commanded always by the greater gust; such is the lightness of you common men.

The destructiveness of the Japanese attack on Pearl made the West Coast fearful that they may be able to do the same to the mainland. Every house in Seattle and probably all coastal cities were equipped with a bucket of sand to fight incendiary bombs, a shovel and a hand pumped water fire extinguisher. An X of regular tape was applied to each window pane to prevent flying glass in case of an air raid. At dark all windows were required to be covered with drawn dark drapes so that no light showed through to the street. There were no street lights and all car headlights had the top half taped over. Every block had wardens that patrolled at night to check for infractions. Man was it ever dark, especially if you had to drive on a rainy night. This was pre-halogen times, so the headlights were dull to start with.

On one foggy night George and I were driving back home from a double date in his dad's 1936 Dodge. Just a typical Seattle night made impossible by no street lights and useless headlights. Coming slowly down University Way there was a thud and a body rolled across the hood. It turned out we had hit two drunken sailors who had been walking down the center of the street. One fell off the side of the car and one rolled clean across the roof. They had both been wearing dark Navy pea coats making them next to invisible. We stopped to help as did the next car behind us, but the third car, due to the fog, failed to stop and hit us both. Makes me think of the song, "What do you do with a drunken sailor early in the morning?" Luckily the sailors were far too relaxed to be hurt so everyone went their way in slightly damaged cars. George and I reported in to the 45th Street police precinct to make a report, but since there was no infraction we were told to go home. Without the benefit of today's cell phones if someone was hurt it might be a long wait before help arrived!

The blackouts and civilian patrols proved unnecessary as the closest the Japanese would get to our mainland was on the outer Aleutian Islands. They did manage to get airborne about 10,000 ingenious incendiary balloons of which nearly 1,000 would reach our coast. Our government at first suppressed information about the balloons as they did not want the Japanese to know they were successful. Over the years about 600 have been accounted for and only a few caused fires. In 1945 a family camping on Gerhardt Mountain in Oregon chanced across one. Not knowing what it was they handled the bomb which exploded killing the mother and her five children. Another fell on wires shorting out the electrical to our secret Manhattan Project in New Mexico. Unfortunately for the world they were still able to complete the A Bomb. The government then decided the public should be informed about the balloons.

There could be as many as 500 remains of these balloons still in our woods with their bombs intact; 265 have been discovered, 40 after the war. The balloons were of paper made from the Mulberry tree used due to its long fibers. Children were used to assemble the balloons because of their soft dexterous hands. The balloons were huge, ten meters in diameter, and 1/3rd lighter than if made from rubber. Earlier balloons may have carried biological weapons into China. They could launch up to 200 a day, each one containing a special prayer, apparently not a strong enough one as they did little damage. This gives further credence to a recent study that prayer only helps the prayer. Filled with hydrogen they travel in the jet stream at up to 30,000 feet making it to our shore in about 60 hours. They rose and fell with the change in temperature; below 15,000 feet sand bags would drop and the balloon would rise. Once over land they released multiple incendiaries. If something went wrong the balloon would self destruct. These balloons were a last effort by the Japanese to hang on in a war the leaders knew they were destined to lose. Even if they had been more successful we were ready, standing brave with our bucket of sand.

With the war came shortages of everything. We only used oil pumped in the USA so the civilian gas supply was short. No more sugar from Hawaii so had to remain friends with Cuba. Not a lot of meat as most went overseas, but it was okay to eat your horse in an emergency. We do not mind eating pigs that cry like a baby when slaughtered, but we do not like eating animals that whinny. Any food like butter that would help grease up arterial shells was in short supply. Margarine was introduced as an alternative, but dairy interests would not allow it to come colored so it came as a pound of what looked like lard with a little capsule of yellow dye which with much kneading would turn it yellow. Unfortunately no matter how hard you kneaded it still tasted like yellowish Crisco.

Big ticket items just vanished; no cars, refrigerators, tires or washing machines. Unlike today where if an item breaks down we just buy a new one, we learned the art of repair and so made do with what we had. If you were lucky enough to have a car and should the tires go bald, you would require the service of a "re-treader." He would rough up the face of your old casing, glue on some new rubber and place it in a mold where the tread pattern would be imprinted and the whole tire vulcanized with heat. If there was a hole in the tires side wall, just put on a patch and use a heavy duty inner tube. One always had to be on the lookout for a worn tire with a decent carcass. I drove a little slower; sometimes. As anyone driving the freeways today can easily see, the art of re-treading has yet to be perfected.

To counter all the shortages there was a weekly curbside pickup of scrap metal, tinfoil, kitchen grease from those lucky enough to have meat or bacon and always newspapers. Everyone had their own government issued coupon book that was needed to purchase rationed items such as meat, sugar and butter. My mother was a master of creative cooking and probably invented "hamburger helper." She never made just a hamburger out of ground meat; instead a pound of meat would turn into a five pound casserole and last several meals. An occasional roast would be served at several meals with the remainder ground, cooked with onions and veggies and then wrapped in bread dough and baked making two more meals. When my mother cooked a piece of meat there was never any red color left and any fat would have melted into the bottom of the pan. She felt you only serve red meat at the zoo. This lack of meat and over cooking may have helped protect the family from future colon cancer. Everyone had enough to eat, but not in excess. The closest we came to fast food might be an occasional can of baked beans. That may be the reason we seldom saw overweight children or adults; diabetes and heart attacks were rare.

The lack of gasoline created its share of problems, especially for someone who had just received his first car. All gasoline was by coupon; A: for most people, B: for those in business and C: for Doctors, emergency vehicles and I am sure politicians. My father, being in what remained of the car business, had a C card and would occasionally find an extra stamp for me. It was easy to get in trouble as the stamp you gave to the station had to match the stamp glued to your back car window. This is when buying all your gas from one local station payed off. Looking back I realize that all the things we liked doing in high school, the PTA dances and going to Shady Beach were dependent on my having a car and access to enough gas. I was the only one of my close friends to own a car in high school.

This was a time that would have made John Kennedy proud when he said, "Ask not what the country can do for you, but ask what you can do for your country." A phrase, unfortunately for many, that Barry Madoff got backwards. We did many inconsequential things that when totaled made a big difference. Women knitted socks and scarf's for those troops in Europe as there were a couple of really cold winters during the war. They also baked and mailed tons of cookies. There is nothing like receiving a homemade cookie when you're on K rations and in a water filled fox hole. Everyone wrote letters and not necessarily to service men they knew. Any letter with news from home was valuable to a lonely man with an uncertain future.

Then there were the USO's manned by volunteers all across the country. They were especially important in the large coastal cities like Los Angeles, San Francisco and New York where men spent their last days before being shipped overseas. It was a place where young men, who often had never before been away from home, could go to talk to non service people, dance with a girl and have a decent meal. They helped allay the fears of young men afraid of what was in their future or if there really was a future. The most famous of the USO's was the Hollywood Canteen where the troops had a chance of meeting the stars. Most female movie stars were generous donating time at the Canteen, while many male stars joined the service. Our unified effort and productive power would prove to be hard for Japan to match till years after the war when we started to import their cars.

Compare our treatment of men going to war in Iraq with WWII. With no draft we depend on repeat visits by inadequately trained "weekend warriors", a few volunteers who join for dubious reasons and mercenaries that cause controversy and seem to be accountable to no one. We show our support for the war by pasting a yellow ribbon on the trunk of our car.

The Victory Garden came into vogue, just like today's pea patch, and people dug up their lawns and parking strips to grow a few veggies. There was little or no sun in our back yard so I borrowed part of my neighbor's back yard. Luckily my family did not have to depend on my home grown veggies to survive. Instead, Mr. and Mrs. Brunner came to Seattle once every week from their farm on Vashon Island with a truck load of fruit, produce, eggs and at times chickens. I am not sure how we got on their route, but my parents may have met them during our summer stays on Vashon. This was the acme of farm fresh organic food and I am sure it contributed to my parent's long life. In spite of rationing and periodic shortages we never seemed to be lacking. Compared to today we had very little, what we did have was designed to last, not to be replaced in a year or two. Even with a war going on I know we were under much less stress, happier and freer than today's children. Dickens's quote could well apply to those years, "It was the best of times; it was the worst of times".

1-45: Soviets take Warsaw and liberate Auschwitz.

2-45: Roosevelt, Churchill and Stalin meet at Yalta in the Crimea.

2-45: Allies bomb and unnecessarily destroy Dresden, Ger.

CHAPTER 11
HIGH TIMES

Sky-lark, have you anything to say to me? Won't you tell me where my love can be? Is there a meadow in the mist where someone's waiting to be kissed?

—Johnny Mercer & Hoagy Carmichael

When the war started I would be in my final year of junior high school at Edmond Meany where I spent two years in seventh and eighth grades. We were the first students to attend this junior high as the program of grade separation was fairly new to Seattle. Previous to this students at Montlake Elementary had spent eight years in grade school. Even in 1940 Meany was old and worn being one of the cities earliest grade schools; an all wood building with oiled wood floors and creaky wood stairs. The physical facility was not as much of a problem for those of us in Montlake as getting to and from school. We were used to walking or riding a bike a few blocks and now had to get to Meany that was one and a half miles away and 600 feet up steep Capitol Hill; walking was out. Biking was possible up the medium grade of Crescent Drive, but it was still a long, tough ride to school, although a quick and exhilarating ride home. That left the bus and a walk of several blocks after debussing. It may come as a surprise to those accustomed to school busing, but we were dependent on the public transit system or more likely on walking. (Let me describe what that is)

This one day a neighbor and also my classmate had taken his bike to school, forgetting he had a later appointment downtown. I was more than glad to help out and ride his bike home as it sure beat walking. I even picked up a passenger Don Jones who also lived near me. I stood up; Don was on the seat as we rode the side streets toward home. Capitol Hill stays flat for about nine blocks on top then drops suddenly at the north end as you start to descend to Montlake. The first short hill was so step it had been paved with cobblestones rather than cement. As we dropped over the edge the coaster brakes failed completely and we immediately gained speed and shot down that first steep hill, across an arterial, Crescent Drive and on down 21st Ave. which led to Interloken Place and a hairpin curve to the right. We were lucky crossing the arterial, but not when we came to the curve. Don thought I was just trying to scare him, which I am sure I did. I never thought of having him slow us by dragging his feet. As we came to the J curve I tried to place the front wheel in the grove where curb meets street in the hope it would slingshot us around the curve. Instead the front wheel wobbled, jumped the curb and threw me thirty feet against a large tree. Don kind of tumbled off the back and slid down the street on his hands and knees. Don damaged his knees, but recovered to play great basketball for Garfield. My bike barely missed a woman gardening in her yard. I was not lucky, receiving a compound fracture of two vertebrae. This put me into a full plaster body cast and later a metal back brace for a total of nine months. I missed the last few weeks of school and to some extent a full summer. Another example of how small events influence one's future and how close I came to possible paralysis.

That summer was spent quietly at our cabin on Vashon Island. Sports activities were out for vertebrae are slow to heal. Of course I could not swim and did no boating as I could not take the chance of melting the plaster cast. The body brace I was fitted for after summer made life much easier, for at least I could remove it for a bath and to scratch, but I felt and looked weird as I entered Garfield for my first year.

Seattle had nine high schools in 1941 and that number stayed steady for years till the "baby boomer era." North of the ship canal there was Roosevelt, Lincoln and Ballard and in the south, Garfield, Franklin and Cleveland. West Seattle was stuck over in the southwest corner of the city so far away they even had to have their own football stadium. Centrally was Queen Ann, atop our highest hill and Broadway, our first and oldest. The school architect had been on a roll so that Garfield, Roosevelt, Lincoln and Ballard all looked about the same. I hear he later went on to design Safeway stores and the milk carton. Franklin was just a little south of Garfield off Rainer Avenue and was a grand classical stone building with large Greek columns marking the front entry. The city later on decided it was way too beautiful so bricked over the front to hide those columns. As I understand it, Broadway was originally designed as a prison, but was converted as the city had no high school at that time. It was built of black stone and was a forerunner to cinder block construction. No one living outside of West Seattle was sure what this high school looked like or where it was. Rumor had it that it once was a large hacienda built by Spanish settlers. If one were to drive south on 23rd Avenue past Garfield and stop at Rainer Avenue the tendency would be to turn south on Rainer to Franklin High, the Franklin Field House and the Sick's Stadium where beer was sold. But, if instead you crossed Rainer and continued south on 23rd it was rumored that eventually you would come to Cleveland High. No one I knew had actually been there and we saw no reason to go look for it. Queen Anne High may have been the nicest of Seattle's high schools architecturally. It sat at the top south end of our tallest hill and commanded a sweeping view of Elliot Bay and Seattle. It later turned out to be much too nice for teenagers so was converted to luxury apartments.

As usual, there were schools for children whose parents did not wish to have their young minds and morals influenced by association with Protestants. That you have to be Catholic to be moral has long since been disproven by the action of their Priests. The poorer Catholic boys attended O'Dea and the wealthier, Seattle Prep. Girls from rich families went to Forest Ridge, poorer to Holly Names and the destitute to Holly Angels on First Hill. Then, there were the private schools; Helen Bush and Lakeside where religion was not involved, only money.

Some families who were really worried about having their child's mind tainted sent their daughters' all the way to Annie Wrights Seminary in Tacoma. During my years in high school I would make friends with boys and girls from all of these schools, mostly by attending dances sponsored by the school's PTA.

For those of us living in Montlake who thought Meany was hard to get to, Garfield was worse. The school was on the same main street that ran through Montlake, but three miles south. The bus ran on this street, but two miles short of Garfield it turned down Madison toward the city center. About half way to town we would debark, walk a few blocks and catch a second bus that took us closer to school. Mostly, the girls took the bus and the boys found it easier to hitchhike as it was a straight shot on the arterial and it had become patriotic to share your ride due to the shortage of cars. Bussing kids all over the city had not yet occurred to our school board so it remained the responsibility of each parent or child to arrive at school on time. I never walked to school due to the big hill, but on occasion we would walk home. Usually if I just stuck out my thumb while walking, sooner or later someone would stop. The fear of car-jacking and mugging would come in later years with Seattle's burgeoning population and increasing number of poor.

On one winter day I had hitched a ride to school, but during the day there was a severe turn in the weather and by the time school was dismissed we had accumulated seventeen inches of snow. For Seattle that means complete paralysis; busses and cars grind to a halt, nothing moves. Those few drivers who went for it usually ended up cross-wise in the street or on someone's lawn. I think they did have sawdust tires, but studs were still in the future. Montlake kids faced a three mile slog home through knee deep wet Seattle snow and in our school clothes. The worst was that I had on my best all leather shoes that were intended for dancing the Avalon, not walking in snow. I made it home cold, wet and frozen.

Known more for its rain, Seattle seemed to have snow every winter. Kids young and old owned sleds and no one was far from a steep, life threatening hill. Thankfully, there were few cars left parked on the street as few owned cars. This helped to keep sledding fairly safe, but occasionally someone would run under a car due to the inability to steer some sleds. I decided I could build the better sled, more along the lines of a toboggan. As a starter I obtained four discarded wood skis from our local Cunningham's ski shop. Using the front half of each ski I built a platform with a steerable front end to which I attached the skis. The city had several days of accumulated snow so I felt this was the opportune time to show my girl friend Sylvia, a skier, my new toy. I wanted to show her that sledding was not just for sissies. Together we dragged the sled to near the top of Capitol Hill. I felt that if it was to be a real test it should be on a big hill; nothing too wimpy. There was one street at the very top that dropped off toward the east side and ran steeply and uninterrupted all the way down to the Arboretum. Even I was a little hesitant when we arrived at the top so we agreed to move our start down one cross street. It took a while to coax Sylvia on to the sled as it did seem a little less sturdy than when it was in my basement. Finally after much procrastination we took off, literally. I was amazed at the sleds acceleration, as was Sylvia who was trying to squeeze the air from my lungs. At the second cross street we became airborne and I began to question the quality of my construction. I knew we were in a bit of trouble when I found the sled would not steer as the skis had no metal edges and were laying flat on the snow. Our only course was straight down the center of the road. Luckily there were no parked cars and I somehow managed to keep the sled centered and did not drift into someone's yard. We zoomed across the bottom cross street into a snow covered berm, shook up, but unhurt. The sled was not as lucky and received severe injuries from which it was never able to recover, much to Sylvia's relief.

High school scholastics were of little interest to me as my overall grade average was only 2.2 upon graduation. I can recall my social life quite clearly, but very little about the classes I attended or the teachers who taught them. I liked wood and metal shop and Mr. Greer who had a gruff demeanor, but was in reality a pussy cat. Courses like chemistry, civics, (especially civics) Spanish and history bored me to tears. I day-dreamed a lot and looked forward to physical education class or to lunch period when I could shoot baskets in the boys gym. Physical education was always my favorite class, but being brought up mostly as an only child I was a little modest about taking the required shower. I felt I should never show my body to a man of my gender as one never knows what could happen. My teachers told me I failed to pay attention; at least I think that's what they said. I hated to stay inside and do home work so I usually put it off till it was too late. My parents told me I pro-crastinated too much. I felt procrastination was not the problem it was the solution. Getting my driver's license at age 16 did not improve my performance, but on the positive side there was little room for my grades to get much worse. I did what was absolutely necessary and did not opt for a lot of additional stuff as I usually had my own agenda.

Lunch hour for the school was split into three periods of thirty to forty minutes each. I would eat my lunch and then spent an hour in study hall taking a nap or rolling marbles down the aisle to irritate the poor teacher in charge; often a substitute. So I requested to be a hall monitor whose job was to help curtail needless running and noise in the halls during lunch time when some classes were still in session. The school made a big mistake here as they probably felt giving me a respon-sible position would help improve my interest in school and so make me a better student; boy, were they wrong. My blond hair and innocent demeanor were deceptive. As Shakespeare once wrote, "O, what may man within him hide, though angel on the outward side." I appreciated the trust and especially that I now could skip dreaded study hall and be rewarded with three lunch periods. I did miss that part of study hall and the teacher's frustration when we rolled those marbles down the long aisles. Most of the time I did my duty, but on occasions when there was a noon dance at Franklin, Lincoln or Queen Ann I would park my car facing down hill about a block from school, rush out a back door to the car as soon as noon period started, coast the car till out of ear shot (small noisy muffler), start up the car and go dancing. Usually one or more of my friends rode along and I am not sure what excuse they used to obtain three lunch periods. If we rushed and sped there was just enough time to drive to another school, have a few dances with our friends and rush back to Garfield. It helped a lot that there was very little traffic, few stoplights and always plenty of parking at the other school. This feat would be impossible in Seattle's present day traffic snarl.

Driving your car during school hour was strictly verboten so it was just a matter of time till I was apprehended and brought up before my peers, the school council. A standard punishment was to have the guilty student help stoke the schools heating system. At this time the school would not be considered green for it was fueled by dirty coal. This was dumped in an interior courtyard and aimed at a manhole in the center. Some went down the hole; the remainder stayed on top and was shoveled down the hole by errant students in an effort to teach them that rule breaking leads to coal shoveling. One other time I was caught smoking during noon time. An alternate punishment in those days was several strokes with a paddle to the butt delivered by one of the members of the student council. Effective punishment and a means of making a point it was used by schools and fraternities. (Much more by frats) Due to the explosion of lawyers counseling has since replaced the paddle. A swat to the butt was quick, lasted only seconds and everyone knew the reason for the punishment. Counseling with an offender just prolongs the problem till no one remembers why they are there.

Smoking is the one thing I sincerely regret having started at age fifteen. As I was growing up it seemed everyone smoked or at least tried it. Magazines and the news papers were full of ads and all the stars in the movies smoked. There was little or no talk about the harmful effects of smoking; although the school coaches seemed to be aware, for a boy athlete caught smoking was kicked off the team. We encouraged men in the armed services to smoke by making sure everyone sent their boys plenty of Butts. The makers of Lucky Strikes did their part by eliminating the packages green dye and saying "lucky strike green has gone to war", as if that would aid the war effort. Considering the spasms that I and others endured in order to learn to smoke I have to ask, why would I want to walk a mile for a Camel? In my years in high school I never saw anyone sell drugs nor did I actually knew anyone that used them. If it had not been for the governments idiotic movie "Reefer Madness" I would never have known what marijuana was. I did have a taste of liquor from a bottle in my parent's cabinet, but could not understand how people could enjoy such a vile tasting liquid. The extent of my high school drinking was maybe a total of five or six beers.

There were few teachers and fewer students who owned cars and drove them to school. All the cars driven to school could be parked on one section of street in front of the school, except for mine which was sequestered a few blocks away waiting for a nooner. Jack, Hap A, Ray J, Ed N, John C and Howie L owned cars and drove them to school at times, but the car I remember the clearest was a mid 1930's LaSalle coupe owned by Jo Anne. That car was just a step below a Cadillac, the bell weather car at that time and a collector car even then.

Garfield was Seattle's only cosmopolitan school. Most students came from middle class neighborhoods such as Montlake, Madison Park and Madrona. There was a poorer section located to the west of school toward down town. The wealthier came from the gated community of Broadmoor or from the Washington Park area overlooking the lake and close to the Seattle Tennis Club. The few black students lived in a small community near 23rd and Madison. Jewish families had settled mostly in the Madrona district where there were several Jewish bakeries. Both Chinese and Japanese student lived toward the older section of Seattle near what was called China Town. Then, as now, there was much speculation as to what the hell actually went on in China Town with its afterhours clubs like the Black and Tan and secret Chinese societies. It was hard for a Caucasian to understand a shop that sold ground Rhino horn, tiger urine and lizard tails. All the Japanese kids were interred about the time I entered Garfield so I never really noticed the disappearance. Many of the Japanese had worked truck farms along the Duwamish River south of town, selling their produce at the Seattle Public Market. Many of these families had bought cars from my father. I am not sure if these students went to Garfield or Franklin to the south. After the Japanese were interred, we decided a better use for their valuable farm land was to cover it with one story warehouses.

Looking back at those high school years I do not remember any real conflict between the ethnic groups and we all seemed friendly at reunions. There was, though, very little intermixing of ethnic groups. I do not remember seeing a Black or Asian couples at any of the PTA dances I attended unless maybe it was an all city dance. Garfield did have its Black heroes; Art Harris and Major Pickford, both staring in football and track. Except for one boy at Broadway High, I do not recall Blacks playing sports in other schools. I do not feel that we as teens were aware of the full extent of discrimination in Seattle at this time.

Most Blacks, Asians and to some extent Jews could not purchase a home in most Seattle neighborhoods. This would slowly change after the war with the huge influx of workers from every part of the country.

On my street in Montlake lived two Jewish families; the Goldberg's with two sons at Garfield and a family directly across from my home with a really cute daughter. At times she would come down and sit on their front steps to watch me shoot baskets at a hoop nailed to the telephone pole. There was a nice mutual attraction, but when I mentioned to my parents about plans to ask her out they made it clear; be friends, but no mixing. I am unsure why it worried them, but children of my age generally gave in to their parents' wishes and I would not do mixed dating till in college.

All children are subjected to the beliefs, prejudices and intolerance as projected by their parents, some more than others. Sad to say, that in my life- time, people throughout the world seem to becoming less and less tolerant of those not sharing their beliefs. Blasphemy laws are on the increase worldwide so in many countries people are fearful of voicing opinions. Solomon Rushdie, in 1989, was sentenced to death by Muslim clerics for writing the "Satanic Verses" in part about the life of Muhammad. A Dane was similarly marked for his cartoon about Muhammad. Jews hate the Muslims, Arabs hate the Blacks, Tutsi the Hutu, Protestants the Catholics and everyone seems to dislike the Jews. No matter what you say someone takes offense.

Most problems arise from overcrowding, lack of knowledge and fear originating from ethnic, religious, gender and color differences. As Adliai Stevenson said when running for president against Eisenhower, "The tragedy of our day is the fear we breed."

Intolerance and a lack of understanding led to what would be my only brush with the law except those few speeding tickets. Or, maybe it was a basic defect as Shakespeare mentions in his introduction to Hamlet:

"So oft it chances in particular men
that through some vicious mole of nature in them,
and by the overgrowth of some complexion
oft breaking down the pale and forts of reason

carrying, I'd say, the stamp of one defect,
Their virtues else be they as pure as grace.
Shall in the general censure take corruption
from that particular fault?

My incident involved this one neighbor in Montlake whose house was only a half block from mine. Their home was the only one in Montlake that was surrounded on three sides by a tall wood fence. The fourth side backed into and blended with the University Arboretum woods. The front entry gate had a small circular design cut into the top so that a person walking by could catch a glimpse of the house, the expansive yard and landscaping all set on a double lot.

The home was occupied by a couple whom I was later to learn were both well respected Seattle attorneys. They were childless and devoted their spare time to their home and garden. They also were known around the city for often riding a tandem bike wearing matching outfits and berets, unusual for those days. Furthermore, there were stories told by their neighbors of having seen the two dancing hand in hand through the adjoining woods in filmy outfits, although I was not a witness to this. They guarded their privacy and had little or no contact with the neighbors. This led people to gossip and make up their own stories, rather like the "Tea Party" today. After all, this is the American way.

I cannot explain why it bothered me or any other neighbor as to what these people did behind their high fence for they harmed no one. In spite of this, one night I and two friends decided we must act. After dark (for who does a foul deed during the day) with paint and brush we wrote nasty words on their front gate, none of which we really understood at that age. Just as we finished another of our friends happened by on his way home and paused to see what we were up to. The next evening the three of us were taken to the central police station for questioning.

One could say that it was a stroke of bad luck that our friend happened by at just the wrong time and later "ratted" us out. To the contrary, being apprehended, like all truths, worked out best for all involved. This was a gentler time and police were not out to prosecute juveniles for some stupid act of vandalism. We worked it out with the couple who had the three of us repaint the front gate and do a number of hours of yard work and leaf raking as restitution. I was rewarded by making friends with two extremely nice people. I would always remember the incident, but it would not now ferment in my conscience for a lifetime. It may be part of the reason I became more tolerant of others beliefs and views, except when it comes to my countries involvement in wars.

I again turn to Shakespeare's Hamlet and what advice Polonius gave to his son Laertes as he was about to return to school:

"This above all, to thyself be true and it must follow as the night to day
that thou cannot be false to any man."

I liked going to school, seeing friends, working with my hands in shop, physical education and sports; I just did not care for the education experience and the boring, rote way it was carried out. Later in life I would read A.S. Neil's book "Summerhill" and realize there actually was a better and less structured approach toward education. A lack of interest in school led to my not participating in extracurricular activities such as planning the year book, the school paper or the yearly Fun Fest. I was not interested in school plays, singing in a choir or playing in the band. I had my own agenda, which was okay, but I missed a lot of activities and interaction with other students. Another reason is that I may have felt slightly intimidated by being around so many over privileged children. My parents did talk me into taking clarinet lessons as we had an instrument left by my brother when he entered the Army. I had visions of being in the band, but I found it as difficult to practice as it was to study and I seemed to blow more squeaks than notes. I could not hide my feelings when my teacher was drafted; boo hoo.

One other reason I may not have been too active in school was that I always seemed to have a job after school. My father like his father before felt it was virtuous for young men to have jobs early so as to have some money of their own. He arranged first for me to work at a book store on Madison in the first hill district that was owned by his fraternity brother. Next I worked for a men's clothier, Bender and Kolstadt, in downtown Seattle, both after school. I cleaned the counters, tidied up and ran errands. I did not like sucking up to people just to make a sale and quit after one year. Working on my first car would lead to a job in auto upholstery where I remained till I finished high school.

By not being active in school affairs I would never really be a part of what was considered the "in crowd" that were on committees, ran for school office or student council. We were friends, but I remained on the periphery. I turned out for basketball, loved to play, but only made the second team as I was never a very good shot. I actually liked all sports, turning out for baseball and track, but disliked staying late to practice so soon dropped out in favor of working on my car, fishing in the arboretum or just playing football in the street with friends. I had even planned to try out for football, but practice started in the fall several weeks before school and I did not care to leave our beach cabin on Vashon early. Life is a series of choices, some good some not so good. As I watched the Garfield Bulldogs play in the mud at the old Civic Field, I was just as happy to be a spectator. Even though I never cared for organized sports I would participate in a variety of sports throughout my life and even today at the age of 80 I still play tennis and ski on a regular basis.

An unfortunate incident cast a pall over one year's football season. Once in a while when Garfield played West Seattle they would hold the game in the West Seattle stadium on a grass field instead of the mud of Civic field. This was looked forward to as it would be the only game on grass and it gave the student body a chance to get out extra early, pile into cars and drive to a game. Since there was no school bussing the few cars tended to be overloaded. After the game the cars were jammed up at the exit waiting to get on the street. One girl was riding in a car trunk with her legs dangling over the bumper when her car stopped suddenly and the car behind did not, crushing both of her legs. My recollection is that she had both legs amputated. A sad end to an otherwise happy school outing.

I developed many friendships of boys and girls from most of Seattle's high schools, but my closest friends from Garfield remained George K., Ray M. and Wayne B. Ray and Wayne are deceased; George still lives in Seattle, while I moved to South Central Washington. We lived near each other in Montlake, but Wayne's parents later moved to Laurelhurst, though he still finished at Garfield. Our weekends during the school year were mostly taken up attending PTA sponsored dances, usually stag, at various locations around the city. There was seldom a weekend that we did not attend two or three dances. At times we might hit an evening dance early and if it remained slow, with few girls; we would hop in the car (usually mine) and speed to another part of town and another dance. We seemed to always know when and where each dance would be held, probably getting schedules from friends in these other schools. We tended to stay mainly with dances in the north end such as those held at the Franklin Field House, Mount Baker Community Center, Margret Tapping's and the Ballard Field House. These seemed to be the best attended.

We loved to dance and we loved meeting new girls and at most of the dances we ended up driving a girl home. At times a new girl, but often someone we already knew. I like to think it was our charm, but it could have been that almost all the girls either walked or took the bus to dances so were usually open to a ride home. Of course, I am sure the girls wanted to meet boys just as badly as we wanted to meet them. We did, over time, get to know a lot of girls that we saw at the dances on a regular basis. Some remained just friends, some we dated and a few we went steady with, but usually not for long as we kept meeting new and interesting girls.

Program dances were especially nice if I was going steady or had a favorite girl, although they were a little more pricey than a PTA dance, often four or five dollars. Social clubs such as Barons or Nobles sold small programs, usually 3X4 inch leather faced, with several pages inside to write the names of people you intended to trade dances with. The club printed up the programs, rented a hall, hired a band and then hoped to sell enough programs ahead of time so as to cover expenses. The program price was called a donation in an effort to avoid paying city taxes and the program became your ticket into the dance. Member's parents usually served as chaperons. High school boys had two rather exclusive "all city" men's clubs; the Ambassadors and the Barons. Originally members were selected from the five north end high schools and tended to be the better athletes', student leaders or just popular kids. I have been told that they originally started as dance clubs, but became more social with time. Later they would draw from all the Seattle high schools. Girls groups like the DAR or the TM's would usually put on a Tolo once a year when girls get to ask out that boy they have been secretly admiring. These dances were well attended as they always had a live band often made up of local high school students. Once a year the PTA and the city would co-sponsor an All City dance held at the Civic Auditorium. They always hired a big name band which helped draw a large crowd. When we all got together at one location you could see just how many teenagers loved dancing the Avalon.

Neither my friends nor I garnered attention from one of these social clubs as we were not active in school affairs nor were we on a sports team. But, as Woody Allen said in the movie Annie Hall, "I wouldn't want to belong to a group that would have me as a member." Somehow we got this "wild and crazy idea" to form our own all city club and put on dances. We gathered all our friends together and formed the "Nobles". Looking back, I am always surprised that we were able to pull it off. What is more surprising is that ten years later all these clubs were still in existence; but no more? I recently called the boys advisor at Garfield High to check on social clubs. There are no longer any social clubs like we had and the advisor was not even aware that there had ever been any, so they must have disappeared quite a while back. He also stated there were neither noon school dances nor any all-city dances that he knew of. I could hazard a guess as to the reasons; inter racial problems, gangs and maybe the type of music today's teens listen to and even increased drug use. Hard to say, but today's teens are missing a lot. I was only in the Nobles long enough to help hold one dance at the Knights of Columbus hall Near Broadway High. I can remember it was touch and go as to whether we would take in enough to cover expenses. I think we just made it by selling a few last minute programs at the door. The reason we did all this was not to make money, but just for the love of dancing. During this era both teenagers and adults could always find a place to go dancing. My father danced his way all through college and belonged to a dance club almost his entire life. Friends I have talked to who were in high school in the 1930's were doing the Avalon, going to Shady Beach and PTA dances every week. Friends who graduated ten years later than I did also were still doing the Avalon and attending

PTA and program dances, but Shady Beach had been sold to the county. So, what happened to that raging interest in dancing? Gone are places like Parkers and the Trianon, not just in Seattle, but all across the country. This lost interest seems to go hand and hand with the introduction of Rock and Roll, the electric guitar and mega amplifiers. Now day's kids do not go to concerts to dance, but only to listen and have their hearing impaired.

Teenage years determine our sexuality; mold our personality and our beliefs. We become the sum total of our experiences; the reason we all turn out a little different, or weird depending on events. As I became a teenager I had no real knowledge of what sex was or what took place between a man and a woman when they went to bed. I did not know what a vagina was as the subject had never come up at dinner. A friend had borrowed his parent's sexual guide that was probably printed during the Gold Rush and I decided I did not want anything to do with what was pictured in that book. Some nights my friends and I would go back in the arboretum and harass lovers as they were making out in parked cars. Some men got really mad, forcing us to run for it, but none of them seemed to be in any position to give chase. I had no idea what rape was, maybe because it was so much less prevalent than today.

That a man might kiss another man never occurred to me yet I did have experience with homosexuality at a young age, but was not really aware of what was happening. One summer I spent several weeks at Cub Scout Camp Meany on Hood Canal. We lived in cabins scattered around the camp; each one with twenty boys and an older Boy Scout as our leader. At one of our night time campfires and while sitting next to my fearless cabin leader I felt this hand sneaking into my pants. I had absolutely no idea what was going on or why anyone in their right mind would want to put their hand into my pants. All I knew was that it did not seem right and it made me extremely uncomfortable. I did not make a fuss in front of everyone, but did make him stop. I confided the incident to my brother who also happened to be a cabin leader. Then it became more of a problem as he was in my brother's class at Garfield where they were both on the track team.

My second "gay" experience occurred one evening after a thanksgiving dinner at my uncles in Bellevue. I was driving my own car as I intended to leave early for a date. My cousin who was a few years my senior asked for a ride back to Seattle. Why not, he lived on Capitol Hill with his parents who were also my Aunt and Uncle. About half way home I found a hand on my knee and suggestions of things that Harvey was sure I would enjoy. If he hadn't been such a creep-----; just kidding. I knew then why my mother was so hesitant when I told her I was giving Harvey a lift. Everyone in the family knew about old Harvey but me. I always knew he was strange, but it was just another subject like sex that we never discussed. I guess she felt that my sexuality was still vulnerable; little did she know.

My lack of knowledge became fully evident when I started dating Marian, a girl I met on a blind date arranged through my friend George and his date. It was a barn dance followed by a hay ride. It was on the hay ride where I discovered how compatible we were. That must be where the "a roll in the hay" originated. We dated some and often arrived at dances alone, but often went home together if neither of us had scored. During a summer hot spell we decided to go swimming after dark at Madison Park Beach. After swimming we spread a blanket on the grass and got into some increasingly passionate kissing. This was the first time I had so much contact with skin on skin and I could feel something was starting to take over my mind. I was more than ready to go all the way right there for due to the mandatory blackout it was pitch dark and no one could make out what anyone else was doing. Marian felt self-conscious with others so close and cooled me down, a little. We drove to her home with our suits still on, but when we parked in front of her house things heated back up and we crawled into the back seat to avoid entanglement with the gear shift. Even the Roman Catholic theologian Saint Augustine of Hippo felt he was under the influence of the devil, for his sexual excitement was not controllable through will power. He said "At times, without intention, the body stirs on its own, insistent; at other times, it leaves a straining lover in the lurch." If Saint Augustine had a problem with control, what chance would I have? I luckily did remembered the words of my health teacher; "do not climax inside a girl." With so little knowledge about sexual matters I have to admit it is best to observe abstinence!

I would have only one other "sexual" experience while in high school and that was with Mona whom I had met at a PTA dance. She was also convenient living just a few blocks away in Montlake. Convenience is a big part of dating; even extending to whom you marry. In the movie Adam's Rib, David Wayne said, "I would love anyone who lived right across the hall from me." Mona was cute, dark haired and passionate with one eye that tended to drift slightly toward her nose. At about this same time I made friends with a boy from Franklin who often talked about his aunt's great home near the Fauntleroy ferry dock that had nice grounds and a swimming pool. He said that his aunt would be gone for a week so if I needed a private place to take a date he would leave the lights on in the pool and house. When we arrived it was just like he said and we made for the pool. I was really beginning to like being next to a girl in a bathing suit and I started get that same sexy feeling I had when with Marian, but Mona also felt too conspicuous in the lighted pool so we went inside and in the heat of the moment laid our wet bodies on this very expensively covered living room couch. Again, my control was no better than Saint Augustine's, except now there was this badly stained couch for which my one time friend would be blamed.

I wasn't about to give up on Mona and since it was summer, Wayne and his date and Mona and I took off for Seaside Oregon for a weekend. We rented one of those old cabins right next to the beach which were at that time affordable to even a high school student. In 1945-46 Seaside was fun, inexpensive and not crowded, which may have been due to price controls or that most men were in the service so business was slow. It was still a small tourist oriented town, funky and low key with various games and entertainment on the main street leading to the Seaside Hotel where there was a go-around so cars could cruise back to where they started or could continue straight down a ramp to the beach. The beach could still be driven on for miles and miles in either direction, but one had better not ignore the tides. We came down early Saturday had a day on the beach, rode the bumper cars, danced, played fascination, ate hamburgers, salt water toffee and had a great time. I went to bed with great anticipation only to find out Mona was having her period. A Chinese proverb says;"a wise man sees his own faults, a courageous one corrects them". I was going to be courageous.

Wayne and I at Sea Side In Oregon

Recently I watched the movie "Charlie Bartlett" on HBO. Made in 2008 it details the problems faced by teens in a modern high school where they face the problem of drugs, abusive or working parents, overcrowding and a lack of self confidence and worth. The movie ends with a play written by one student who had earlier tried to commit suicide; "Hell Comes with Your Own Locker". Is high school really hell now? All movies exaggerate, but there was this thread of truth that ran through the movie and it saddened me to think how much more difficult it is for a teenagers in today's world than when I was a teen. We had it so good; maybe some of the best times of our life. Consider this poem by Nixon Waterman about how a child grows up:

> Hurry the baby as fast as you can,
> Hurry him, worry him, make him a man.
> Off with his baby cloths, get him in pants,
> Feed him on brain foods and make him advance.
> Hustle him, soon as he's able to walk,
> into a grammar school; cram him with talk.
> Fill his poor head full of figures and facts,
> Keep on a-jamming them in till it cracks.
> Once boys grew up at a rational rate,
> Now we develop a man while you wait,
> Rush him through college, compel him to grab
> Of every known subject a dip and a dab.
> Get him in business and after the cash

All by the time he can grow a mustache.
Let him forget he was ever a boy,
Make gold his God and its jingle his joy.
Keep him a-hustling and clear out of breath,
Until he wins—nervous prostration and death.

Hard to believe it was written around 1859.

4-12-45: President Roosevelt dies; Harry Truman takes over.

4-30-45: Hitler commits suicide.

4-7-45: Germany surrenders; V.E. day.

CHAPTER 12
VASHON ISLAND

Go-na take a sentimental journey, Go-na set my heart at ease, Go-na take a sentimental journey to renew old memories. Got my bag, got my reservation, spent each dime I could afford, like a child in wild anticipation, wait to hear that all aboard.

—Brown, Homer & Green

Everyone has this special place during their youth where they were happiest; mine was a bare-bone cabin overlooking the west channel that lay between Vashon Island and the Kitsap Peninsula in Puget Sound. The cabin was perched on a sandy bank and set back twenty feet from a four foot bulkhead that protected it from high tides. The cabin was close to the north end of the island, maybe two to three miles from the ferry landing. The cabin itself rested on concrete piers and was basic 2X4 frame construction with only shiplap siding on the exterior. Bare studs were exposed on the inside and there were many gaps in the siding that provided excellent ventilation, but had to be plugged with rolled up newspaper when the weather turned nasty. The interior was about 20 feet square with one third divided between the kitchen and a dressing room. The kitchen held a full size, four burner cast iron wood burning stove, a tank for hot water and a sink and drain board. The stove did triple duty, providing cooking, warmth and our hot water but presented a problem on hot days when preparing dinner or if water was needed for a shower. Perishable food was stored in an ice-box that sat on a small back porch off the kitchen. A large block of ice was loaded into a top compartment once a week by the iceman.

This interior cabin area was surrounded on two sides by a ten foot wide porch that was screened for privacy and divided into sleeping areas by sheets hung on wires, leaving a central part for sitting and eating outside if the cabin became too hot. Adjustable white canvas awnings hung on the outside and could be raised and lowered to protect the porch from the sun's late afternoon glare off the water at high tide. In a corner of the porch near my bed was a small 3X3 foot shower that could be either warm or cold depending on the state of the stove.

The "bathroom" was about thirty feet of sand away from the back kitchen door. A basic frame, single seat structure over an eight foot deep hole dug in the sand. When the odor became too intense we would dose the hole with lye and with an extra dose in the fall when closing up the cabin. If after a year or two the lye failed to solve the problem or the dung came to close to the seat, the owner, Mr. Land, would dig a new hole a few feet away and use the excavated sand to fill the old hole.

At one time this section of beach had been a sand and gravel oper-ation and contained maybe 3000 feet of waterfront. They had used high pressure hoses to wash down sand and gravel from the steep hill sides and were now left with a large flat sandy expanse on which the owners built rental cabins. The cabins, except for ours, were built against the back hill about 100 feet from the water's edge to take advantage of the banks shade trees. The large sandy expanse was free of trees except for several Madronas' which are able to grow in sand. The ground rose steeply in back of the cabins and continued steeply and wooded for maybe a mile to the main road which ran down the middle spine of the island. When the sand and gravel operation ceased, the property was divided between two sisters and so became Corbin Beach and Land Beach, our cabin being on Land's.

The steep wooded land behind the cabins held our "organic" water supply. The ground was alive with small springs so to access the water

Mr. Land had driven a series of perforated pipes into the side of the hill. These pipes fed into ten or twelve large interconnected wooden barrels with window screening on top to keep out leaves and debris. From there it was piped to each cabin, free from chlorine, fluorine, additives or health inspectors; maybe an occasional bug. No one ever thought of questioning the waters purity and to my knowledge it never made anyone ill. I do not remember ever running short of water and there was a continual overflow that fed a small stream running through a lush garden tended by Mr. Land's mother. Affectionately known as "Grama Land", she lived alone in a tiny cabin and had created this oasis from a patch of sand. Grama was a character right out of a Norman Rockwell painting. This lush garden resulted from a combination of water and an endless supply of fish remains that we kids brought to her and which she buried next to her favorite plants. She had over the years created soil out of sand, compost and fish entrails in an area where only scotch broom, a few wild flowers and a very sharp edged sedge grass managed to survive.

While my parents lived in Tacoma they had become good friends with the Middleton's who had been renting one of Corbin's' cabins for several years. They in turn talked my parents into taking an available cabin on Land's side. During the first few years of renting we were up against the back hill which tended to be a little damp as the hills were full of springs. When the beach front cabin became available we took it over and remained there for many years. Each year a few cabins would change hands, but the present renter always had first choice and most returned for many years. The rental amount never varied; $125.00 a year for a cabin on what was probably the best beach on Vashon. Both owners were laid back and easy to get along with. A renter could pretty well make any improvements at their own expense. A few that knew they were there for the long haul put in septic tanks, inside toilets and siding to keep out the wind. Even though we rented for years we stuck with the original building, newspaper in the cracks and more lye in the outhouse. If there was some small repair to make it was better to find a way to do it yourself as Mr. Land was not exceptionally prompt. My mother liked to kid about the time she asked Mr. Land to fix a leaky faucet in the shower near her bed as the drip kept her awake at night.

He came down and tied a string from the shower head to the floor so the water could run down quietly.

Earlier renters at both beaches along with help from the owners had built two clay tennis courts. They had dug the clay from boggy areas in the hill behind the cabins and carefully pressed and stomped it in place. Tall cedar poles held up wire at each end. Each spring the winter's damage had to be repaired with new clay dug from the hills. The clay required watering several times a week to keep it from drying and cracking. The courts were reserved for the adults on evenings and weekends, but this is where my friend Jack Kidder and I first learned to play tennis while the men were at work. On certain occasions, like Fourth of July, the two beaches would play challenge matches as part of the celebration. Over the years as the complexion of the beach changed, tennis players disappeared and were replaced by baseball lovers. Down came the wire screen at one end and the court became a diamond. The outfield was part sand bank and part scotch broom and sloped toward the water making it a challenge to catch a fly while running up hill through brush. It all worked out for both Jack and I also loved to play baseball.

There were young children in most of the cabins requiring the women to stay at the beach full time. Men were still the only ones that worked in most families, but the war did start to draw more and more women into the work force. Some men commuted on the ferry mostly as walk-ons, a few drove cars. There was a path from the ferry dock, through the woods and then along private bulkheads to our beach and continued on farther south to more homes. No one ever complained if you crossed their property. If driving, after leaving the ferry you climbed to the islands highest point and took one of the first roads to the right. The road down to the beach was loose gravel and dropped precipitously following a natural ravine through twists and hairpin turns for about a mile. Many portions of the road had room for only one car so it was best to honk at each sharp curve. Near the end of the summer the road became wash boarded so it was best to go slowly or risk bouncing right off the edge.

When we first started to stay at the beach the mosquito fleet still operated the Virginia V commuter down the west channel. It started from the down town Seattle water front, taking men home at night and picking them up in the morning. There was a whole series of docks spaced at intervals down the west channel. The Sylvan Dock was ours and was just a five minute walk from our beach. The dock did double duty as our fishing pier where we caught perch and cod. I am not sure why the service was discontinued, but it was probably for the same reason they abandoned the interurban rail line; road building followed by an increased use of the automobile. Considering the present cost of a ferry ride, I am sure many Vashon residents would love to have the old commuter boats back.

When I finally was able to drive I often took my car to the beach. From Montlake it was about a half hour drive to the Fauntleroy dock with seldom a waiting line. The cost was about $.75 cents for car and driver. The ferries were small and would look like toys alongside today's mega-ferries that hold hundreds of cars. The only time there would be a line was if you came back to Seattle Sunday evening. Then you might have to wait for the second boat.

In spite of the outhouse and the wood stove my mother loved the beach as much as I did. Some of her best friends stayed at the beach all summer and there was seldom a day or an evening after dinner that they did not get together, usually at Middleton's, to play bridge or just talk. Most of the husbands, like my father only came over on weekends. Families, like us, did not have a car at the beach, but depended on once a week deliveries for our groceries and ice. Groceries mainly came by car from the store at Vashon Heights' and were ordered using the only phone on the beach; a hand cranked one at Grama Lands'. There was also a grocer at the ferry landing, but his deliveries were by a barge powered by a huge cranky old 50 HP outboard. There were no electric starts yet so it was always touch and go to get the big ones running. Additionally, the barge had a hard time landing on our beach due to the long tidal run out. When the ice man "cometh" each week it was important to stuff the box full, for during hot weather it was hard to make a load last the seven days. On rare occasions we were treated to a ride into town with one of the few women with a car. This often became necessary to get gas for my outboard. We never thought that we were isolated, just slightly inconvenienced. No one would have given up their cabin for those reasons. There is something rather peaceful in knowing that you cannot be reached by every person you know every minute of every day. I like the first stanza from the poem "Far From the Maddening Crowd" by Nixon Waterman:

> It seems to me I'd like to go where bells don't ring, nor whistles blow,
> Nor clocks don't strike, nor gongs sound, And I'd have stillness all around.

It was not all fun and games; I was the chief supplier of wood, bark and kindling to keep the fire burning so mother could prepare meals. Cooking on a wood stove did not cause mother's cooking to suffer; instead I felt it made food taste better. Supplying wood for the stove would have been easier if the chainsaw was available, but hard work gives one a glow that you would never get from using a chainsaw. Instead, I settled for a two man crosscut saw operated by just one boy. I like to feel the hard work developed character besides muscle. The logs we preferred to cut up had broken loose from log booms being towed up the west channel to mills near Seattle. It was illegal to cut up these logs as they were all marked with a brand and periodically a tug would come around at high tide looking for them as they still belonged to the mills. That means we had to cut and split fast in order to avoid possible detection. I must have had a streak of larceny that was surfacing at a young age.

Everyone at the beach loved to gather bark as it burned hot and slow. It occasionally came floating by in huge drifts, especially after very high tides. Everyone with a boat would row out and fill up to the point of sinking. Though it burned great it had a high salt content and raised havoc with the stove and pipes, which often rusted out after just a few years. Luckily with the extensive electrification carried out during the depression years it was easy to find replacement wood stoves.

Kindling to start the fire had to be cedar and was not always easy to find. I was forever on the lookout for cedar and would test every old or new log on the beach with an axe and my nose. Finds' were kept secret, cut up and brought home fast. In all the years of splitting fire wood and chopping kindling I only tried to chop off one finger. Cutting kindling one day I was amazed to see the end of my left first finger hanging on by a bit of skin. I quickly re-attached it with a few wraps of adhesive tape and kept on chopping. It's a little numb to this day, but functional.

I did not take to the water easily as it took me a long time to find out the difference between sink and swim. When I finally learned to swim I became eligible to have a boat. My father purchased the boat from the Fletcher family who had decided to not re-rent their cabin. Getting a first boat is an event on par with getting my first car as it opened horizons not obtainable from land. It was a standard 12 foot; Grandy built row boat commonly seen at that time. It was flat bottomed, cedar planked and with seats in the stern, mid-section and bow. The exterior was white; the interior green, standard boat colors for those days and it came with a set of heavy oak oars. It cost all of $15.00 which today would not even buy one of the cedar planks. My friends Jack K. and Doug W. had the same boat and we all did a lot of rowing which helped build strong arm and back muscles. I later felt that the rowing helped me to recover from my broken back and led to many trouble free years.

Me Jack and Doug

I loved rowing, but an outboard motor greatly extends one's range. Unfortunately, as with cars, the war brought a halt to the production of new outboards. Jack K. was the only one at the beach to own a newer 1941 Johnson, 2 ½ HP with a recoil starter. Luckily, his father had bought it just before the start of the war. My father searched for a used motor and finally found a 2 HP, one cylinder, 1928 model Johnson that probably should have been in the Smithsonian. It had an exposed flywheel on which you wrapped a rope on each attempt at a start, which could be numerous during one of its stubborn periods. It was not quite as fast as Jack's newer 2 ½ HP motor or Doug's older 4 HP. As a result I would be left behind when they took longer trips and did not want to slow down for me. I would be momentarily sad, but there was a lot to keep me busy. All during the war we searched for a newer, more powerful engine. I obtained at least three that needed repair, but could never get one to run as replacement parts were nonexistent. I failed to get a newer engine, but I did learn a lot about engines; knowledge that became valuable when I got my car.

That cranky old engine took me to a lot of places and never failed to bring me home. Fishing for Cutthroat Trout was my number one pastime. I caught them to eat as they were by far the best tasting fish. These trout were plentiful around the north end of Vashon due to swift tides, small streams and a lot of undeveloped shoreline. At high tide the fish came in to feed right near the bank and under the overhanging brush. They are voracious feeders and will strike at almost any small lure trolled behind the boat. I traveled up and down the west channel searching for the best spots. When I found one, I would remove the motor from the stern, stow it in the bow and row while fishing. I caught a lot, for at that time there was no limit; I imagine that I and others like me helped contribute to the present species decline.

My constant companion while either boating or while on shore was a small brown cocker named Budge. At least the top half resembled a cocker with long ears and a stub of a tail. On the bottom were four short stubby bowed legs more likely found on a Dachshund. To my surprise, recently while watching the Westminster Dog Show I saw a dog win best in show and he is the spitting image of my dog Budge. The original owners claimed he was a pure bred; maybe they were right. My family had not done well with pets in past years. A small terrier was accidently killed with a worm overdose. A grey Persian got pregnant and had a litter in a barrel of wrapped dishes in the basement and was later found dead in the gutter of our main arterial. When one of our neighbors said he knew a dog that needed a home, my parents were a little reticent to try again, but I convinced them that he would be my responsibility. The neighbor took me over to Vashon Island in the rumble seat of his Packard convertible where I had a choice between Chester and Budge. Budge and I bonded and became the boy and his dog.

We both loved the out- of-doors whether on Vashon or in the Arboretum in Seattle. For a dog with such short legs he was tireless and would endlessly chase a ball or any other animal that chose to run. He was small of stature, but not of courage and would fight any male dog regardless of size, usually while lying on his back. He was also over sexed and tried to mount any female he came across who was in heat. It never occurred to us that we should have him neutered as it was not a common practice at that time. I am sure there were a lot of weird looking puppies with short legs that we knew nothing about. I always looked at his attempts to mate as humorous rather than creating unwanted animals. I do know better now and all sixteen of my rescued dogs and cats are fixed. Dogs become an integral part of a family, are adored and often given human qualities. I like the joke where two dogs are talking and one says: "When we do bad things, people blame themselves; when we do good, WE get praised—are we Gods or what!"

My boat was built for function and even though out of cedar was quite heavy for one boy to get into the water when the tide was low. To help, I kept three round pieces of logs that I placed in a row under the boat. This allowed me to easily drag the boat to the water without removing all the bottom paint. As soon as the boat was at the water's edge Budge was in and perched on the bow seat with his front feet on the stem. With the motor on full his ears stood out like wings. Occasionally if I turned sharp to avoid a drift he would tumble overboard and I would have to grab him by the collar as he went by and pull him back on board. I do not feel he was always thrilled by the long hours in the boat, but it would have been hard to leave without him. I know he enjoyed exploring the expanse of woods that lay between the beach and the island highway. Every now and then he would give chase to a deer and it could be two to three days before we saw him again. He always managed to find his way home. Together we covered most of the west channel, caught a lot of Cut Throat and explored a lot of land that had yet to be populated.

On one late afternoon we attempted to assist some people walking the beach and who had become stranded at the north point and could not make it back to the ferry due to a very high tide. They had walked

along the beach and did not pay attention to the rising water which
when high came up two or three feet against a steep bank. Budge and
I, being good Samaritans, offered to take them to the bulkhead close to
the ferry landing. There were four adults and I could see they were a little awkward when getting in the boat. They were more awkward getting
out as one woman put her full weight on the gunnel pushing it under
water and sinking the boat. Everyone ended up as wet as if they had
walked back.

Vashon summers were like belonging to a large extended family that
held a three month reunion once a year. Most families returned year
after year even after their children were grown and had left home.
Several couples who also lived in Seattle became close friends and were
seen year around by my parents. Occasions like Labor Day and Fourth
of July were celebrated together by both beaches. While the tide was
low the children competed by age in speed, potato sac and three legged
races. The big boys had a rowing race and the two beaches challenged
each other at tennis, baseball and horseshoes, which ever was in vogue.
The egg toss was open to all and always produced a lot of laughs. After
dark everyone came to a huge bonfire for songs and entertainment. On
the Fourth the men would shoot off an incredible array of fireworks as
we all roasted marsh mellows. That secure feeling of community was
important to children and adults, but was often missing when returning
to the city.

When my aunt Lettie's financial situation became critical we moved
her to Seattle to live with us full time. When she was at the beach we
screened off a small additional section of the front porch for her bed.
Even though she had spent her entire adult life living alone she easily
blended in not only with us but with all my parent's friends. The three
of us spent many an evening playing three handed bridge as they taught
me the intricacies of the game. This knowledge served me well years
later at my fraternity where several bridge games were going on 24/7.
Lettie was not in the best of health and was plagued by arthritis. She
took a large number of aspirins each day to counter the pain as this was
the best medication available at the time. Unfortunately it led to sub-
cutaneous and internal bleeding throughout her body. Sadly she was
with us only about ten years before passing on.

My contribution to the war effort was catching as many dogfish as possible, take out their livers and sell them at $5.00 a pound to the government. Dogfish are not exceptionally big, but one third of the weight is in the liver. I never had much love for them for they seemed to be everywhere and continually took my bait when fishing near the bottom for cod. I felt no pangs when slicing one open to get at the liver, but was always vigilant of that poisonous spine near its tail as they could nail you with it even when in the throes of death. It always amazed me when I opened one up and there would be several fully formed baby dogfish inside with a small yellow sack hanging down to sustain them for a short time after birth. I turned them free even though I knew they would be back later to steal my bait. First I would catch or spear small fish like sole, cut them into pieces and bait up to one hundred hooks on a trot line. The baited line was then dropped out in the deep and left overnight when dogfish are more active feeding. I was gung-ho for a while, but it soon became more work than pleasure. Any line with a hundred hooks is constantly tangled and I was forever sticking a hook somewhere into my body. Also the can of livers were starting to smell bad as I could not catch dog fish fast enough to fill the can and the icebox was too small to hold them. I finally cashed in about three gallons of livers and have never been sure what it was they were used for.

When I was not fishing or cutting fire wood I was in the forest behind the cabins. In washing out the sand and gravel they had left a large fairly flat area that was now overgrown with alders and wild blackberries. The high hill was undercut leaving a vertical section to the top that could only be scaled using an old ship's boarding ladder put up by previous explorers. The last twenty feet led to our "pirate's lookout" as we were able to see out over the trees all the way to the Kitsap Peninsula.

Jack K. got the urge to build a log cabin in this flat area so one day started to chop down a series of large alders. This was okay with Mr. Land as the alders had no real value and if downed it would allow firs to grow. I had to check out what he was up to and found he had already felled a few trees and laid logs for the cabin's base. I didn't want Jack to hog all the fun so pitched in with my axe as it seemed like a great project, though neither of us had felled trees before. Jack's brother Bill had prepped him a little so that he knew enough to use an undercut to point the tree in the direction he wished it to fall. It was hard work, for our only tool was the axe. It was harder yet to get a log over to the cabin and hoist it into position as the wall got higher. I think finally we decided that the real fun was in felling the trees and we soon forgot about the cabin. Together we cleared a large area and turned it into a jumbled mess of fallen alders, but a great future area for blackberries. Amazingly, we managed to escape without hitting each other with a tree. I don't think either of our parents had any idea what we were doing up in the woods. Both Jack and I did a lot of things on both land and water that could be considered dangerous, but our parents never showed extreme concern or tried to limit our activities. I think they felt that the adventures we had were a part of growing up and if you made it you would be much the better for it. We're still debating that.

Jack, like his older brother Bill, was a good athlete, strong and well coordinated. When we were a little younger he and I and all the other kids at the beach would congregate after dinner, draw out a large circle in a flat sandy area and play "cut the pie." That is, when we were not playing baseball. Jack was always the best. One thing about Jack was that he always wore leather moccasins on bare feet while I wore a laced up tennis shoes. I tried the moccasins once, but could never figure out how to keep them on. Jack must have had sticky feet. At Garfield he excelled at football, track and basketball. He was willing to leave the beach early, or stay after school for practice. He went away to college and I lost track of him, I only know he become a teacher.

If I was not out in the boat or swimming I was off walking along the beach or through the woods. With the tide out we could walk the beach to the north point near the ferry dock or south to Fern Cove where there was a small stream. The path through the woods led to the ferry and at the very end of the dock was a tiny restaurant that served home-made wild blackberry pie alamode; Yum, yum. Because the banks on Vashon are steep and come down right to the water's edge, most homes were built on land created with wood bulkheads. To get around at high tide it was always necessary to walk on some ones bulkhead. No one ever said get off or stopped others from digging clams in front of their home.

Years later I answered an ad for a summer rental on Vashon and it turned out to be two houses down from Land's beach. I was able to do the same things with my children as I had done. Land's half of the beach had changed very little and I went up to say hi, finding that they still charged $125 a year. In contrast the Corbin half had been subdivided and sold to the renters and had been turned into a Seattle subdivision with full time homes. I no longer felt comfortable walking thru their property, but was slightly intimidated and stayed to the beach even though I had been friends with most of the owners at one time. I also took my kids through the woods where Jack and I had tried to build that cabin and guess what, no Alders, but lots of tall Fir trees.

I turned sixteen, received my driver's license, got my first car, was working, dating more girls and dancing the Avalon as often as possible. It was getting increasingly more difficult to find time to go to the beach. I did not just stop, but needed to work to support my car and dating, so started going out evenings or some weekends. Also, there was Sundays at Shady Beach which started to take priority. Luckily, even though Fauntleroy was a drive, it did not take very long to get there from either Montlake or whereever I was working. Gas was still only 15 to 17 cents a gallon and the ferry was cheap. So, if I had the time, cost was no factor and I still went to the beach often. My job payed about $.85 cents an hour which seems like a small pittance by today's wages, but I always felt I had plenty of money to do what I wanted. It always amazed me in later years that even though my wages increased my buying power kept decreasing. I do recall my parents helped pay for some of my gas as I was able to charge at Cherbergs station in Montlake.

During the last few years that we rented the beach cabin, Vashon played an important role in my dating. When my friend George and I attended Montlake Grade School one of our class mates lived a block away on my street and close to George. He was bigger than either George or I and looked and acted older. He had a deeper voice and had a tendency to be somewhat of a bully. I often passed his house on my way home and was a little fearful when he was outside looking down on me from his terraced lawn. I was never quite sure if I was going to get past his house unscathed so finally chose to take an alternate route home. In music class the teacher would often take hold of his hair and pull up in an effort to have him sing higher. It did not work. About the same time that I entered high school, he and his family moved to

Vashon Island and for some reason remained in touch with George. I, on the other hand was happy to see him move, for I could now walk my street un-threatened. When we were juniors in high school our friend invited George for a visit and while there introduces him to his 14 year old cousin Joan. Joan was a little young, but seemed mature and was one of the best looking girls I would ever meet. It was fall and we were back in school, but George had no car of his own and Joan was too young to go to Seattle on her own. But, Roger has a car and even access to a cabin that lies directly across on the other side of the Island from where our friend and Joan lived. Coincidentally, Joan had a slightly older red headed sister named Ann. You may be able guess the rest.

George fixes me up with Ann and in return gets a ride to Vashon; it's a win, win situation. The girls lived a mile from the ferry dock but to reach the their home we would park at our friend's house and then take a dirt trail that had been dug out of the hill side and that angled down toward the beach for maybe a quarter mile. It was well shaded and hidden with brush and overhanging trees, much like a tunnel. It became a real challenge to navigate at night without a flash light. Their house was rather small and rustic, probably intended to be used only as a summer home. It rested in a scooped out flat area twenty or thirty feet above the beach, surrounded by vegetation. Half the house was two stories with bedrooms above overlooking the living room and kitchen area. There was a nice fireplace with a couch in front. This couch was where we spent some of our time perfecting our necking technique and where Ann, a little older than I, taught me how to properly kiss a girl, for which I am eternally grateful. Her solution to kissing was simple; just say prunes as you started each kiss. I don't know why I hadn't thought of that.

One weekend I was staying at the beach with plans to attend the Saturday dance at Burton near the south end of Vashon with Ann. I drove over to my friend's house, but he wanted to take his car so Ann and I rode in the rumble seat of his Model A coupe. The roads on Vashon pretty well followed the property lines so there are a number of right angle corners. He hit the first left curve way to fast causing the car to tilt precariously onto the two right tires. This was followed by a few screams and a lot of bad language. I am not sure what kept the car upright, maybe another divine intervention. Being in the rumble seat, I doubt if Ann or I would have survived a rollover. We managed to make it to the dance where there were mostly island boys who soon let me know that they did not take kindly to "big city" kids going out with their local girls. They did not want to dance with the local girls, but they did not want any outsider to dance with them. The dance was fun even though no one on Vashon, including Ann, knew how to dance the Avalon.

When we were ready to go home my friend was nowhere to be found so Ann and I had to settle for a ride with two locals that Ann knew. It was a drive to remember as the driver set out from the start to scare me. I will have to admit he did a great job. I guess Ann was more used to their crazy driving for she stayed calmer. The driver sped down the back roads which at that time were mostly graveled making the car very skitterish on curves. They drove at what seemed to me to be a high speed and then would turn off the car headlights for a few miles. I was trying to squeeze the juice out of anything I could grab hold of. I was not able to see a thing, but as it turned out they knew their roads for we soon ended up where I had left my car, shaken, but safe. This was my first and last Burton dance with Ann; the locals had me convinced.

We did on occasion go to the town of Vashon to see a movie. Other than the Burton dance and speeding blindly down back roads, this was the island's only other form of entertainment. The theater was a really old wooden building and could get a little crazy with teenagers on weekends. Most seats were regular old wood theater type except for the back two rows. This was referred to as "the loge "and consisted of old auto bench seats. The high school kids vied for these seats so they could get in a little necking or sneak a few smokes during the movie. One weekend a fire started in the loge area where our friend loved to sit and the theater burned to the ground. They never did find out who was to blame for starting the fire. I was not present so can only speculate. Our friend, in years to come, really settled down going into business with his father and to my amazement in later years was elected mayor of Vashon; turning out to be not only popular, but competent.

We had very little contact with Ann and Joan's parents. Their mother had a wonderful sense of humor and often talked about writing a book and even intimated that George and I would be in it somewhere. It was after we had stopped seeing the girls that "The Egg and I" was published, but that was about her life on a chicken farm on the Olympic Peninsula. Her great sense of humor showed up in that first book; one of the funniest I have ever read. Her next book "Onions in the Stew" was about her life on Vashon and may have included a reference to teenagers that resembled George and Me.

While living on Vashon during the summers it was almost impossible to tell our country was at war. At times there was a P.T. type craft stationed at the ferry landing, but with no torpedoes. Occasionally we saw it speed down our channel on some sort of rescue mission. It may have picked up downed flyers as P-38's used to scream by just a few feet above the water and we heard rumors of crashes. Once a naval vessel, possibly a destroyer, came down the west channel a little too fast at high tide and washed out a number of bulkheads. Blake Island off the north end was used for loading munitions and was restricted for civilians and pleasure boats. Since our demands were rather meager we never noticed shortages. Except for the small amount of gas I used in my outboard, most of what we required was grown or raised right on the Island. Since there was a labor shortage the Island kids including those from our beach helped pick the berry and fruit crops for which Vashon was known and in the process earned a little spending money.

My family's time on Vashon was nearing an end. Even though we had rented from Land's my family was offered 100 feet on the Corbin side when the property was divided. They did not care for the piece they were offered so turned it down. In some ways it was a mistake; for a few thousand dollars they could have had desirable waterfront property that later became hundreds of times more valuable. This is another example of those decisions that influence the course of one's life, sometimes for the better, sometimes the worse, who's to say? My interests were more and more directed toward cars, girls and dancing and I found less and less time for the beach. With my aunt Lettie gone, mother would have been there alone most of the time so my parents decided to also give up our rental. What I learned from my time on Vashon was individualism, self reliance and inventiveness besides how to kiss and play bridge. Oh, I almost forgot; I learned to be nice to older people, once they were you and soon you will be them. I never was much for looking back; adios amigo, aloha Shady Beach

7-45: 1,000 bomber raid on Japan; Japan says they will fight on till the end.

7-45: First ever test of an A bomb in Nevada desert; Arrival of the nuclear age.

7-26-45: A Bomb "little boy" sent to Tinian Island on cruiser Indianapolis.

7-45: Indianapolis later sunk with a loss of 881 men. (tit for tat.)

CHAPTER 13
CARS, CARS AND MORE CARS

Let' take a boat to Bermuda—Let's take a plane to Saint
Paul—Let's take a kayak to Quincy or Nyack, Let's get away
from it all—Let's take a trip in a trailer—no need to come
back at all—Let's take a powder to Boston for chowder—Let's
get away—

> —Tom Adair & Matt Denns,
> —First recorded by T. Dorsey & F. Sinatra

There is one thing that has not changed from my generation to today's; the excitement a teenager feels when getting their first car. Of course our cars were a far cry from the "starter cars" a teen might receive today. I would turn sixteen during the war after new car production had ceased for over a year. This put a heavy demand on used cars so that they soon became hard to find, expensive and not always in very good condition. I was luckier than most kids my age for my father worked at the S.L. Savidge Dodge and Plymouth agency located at that time on Broadway Avenue and John Street near Broadway High School. In 1941 most Seattle car dealers were located in this area.

My dad saw nothing wrong with teens driving and had groomed me

My First Set of Wheels,
Tacoma, WA.

for several years to be a safe, responsible driver. My introduction to driving started when I was still young as I sat in my father's lap and steered the car on our way to Sunday School at the Episcopal Church on East Denny Way. Brittney Spears would later be admonished for a similar incident, but it was okay in the 1930's. My mother having descended from sturdy Church of England stock insisted on children having proper religious indoctrination; a trait inherited from earlier times when the church was under the thumb of the Pope. I resisted as there were important things Budge and I had to do in the Arboretum, but I acquiesced knowing that I would get to steer the car. Over time I graduated from merely steering to both steering and shifting the early cars with three on the floor. By age fifteen my legs were long enough to reach the clutch and brake pedals and I received further driving instruction from my father. We stayed on deserted back streets as there were yet no mega market parking lots to practice on. I slowly mastered that delicate balance between clutch, brake, and shift and soon was able to watch the road and manipulate the levers without crossing the curb or ramming a parked car. By the time I would turn sixteen I was confident in my mind, like all teen drivers, that I was easily one of the better drivers in Seattle and clearly capable of having my own car.

Unbeknownst to my parents I had actually had much more practice driving than they realized. Now that my parents are deceased I can confess to borrowing the family auto on nights when they were out dancing, which was fairly regular. My father drove a company used car to and from work and would use it on evenings so as to save our gas so my mother could use the car in the day and I could practice driving on some nights. My father had predicted the new car shortage so had bought a 1941 Dodge with something new called "fluid drive" just as the war started. I could never drive very far for fear they would notice the change in gas level, but then who really remembers how much gas they have left? Mostly I drove the car locally with friends. A few times we would visit girls and impress them with how cool we were to have access to a car at such a young age.

There was one time on that proverbial cold and stormy night after my parents had left for their dance that George and I decided to extend our range by driving what to us was far out to the roller rink on north Aurora Avenue. My parents had left early and I was sure they would not return till 11 PM, giving us lots of time. It was a stormy night, but I had no problem until approaching the Montlake Bridge as we returned home. At this time the bridge surface was still brick and George mentioned that if you gunned the engine while on the bridge the wheels would spin. I gunned it, the tires lost traction, spun and we did a 180 shooting out the other end of the bridge backwards and slamming hard into the curb. Luckily in those days there was seldom any night time traffic so we suffered no body dents, only this hole in the side of one tire. It was time for deception. We changed the tire, put it in the trunk with the hole down and re-garaged it. The following day my neighbor Remi, who had a car, took the tire to a re-treader who did a masterful job of cementing a hunk of rubber over the hole. We returned it to the trunk, hole facing down, and no one was the wiser. Luckily they never had to use it as patches in the side wall were unreliable. To unburden my conscience I would confess when I was in my forties; good for the soul, though my parents doubted I had one. When I later had children there was no way they would outwit me for I knew all the tricks. Never underestimate the cunning nature of a child, when they became adults it was their turn to confess to me.

My first car would be a 1930 Ford Model A two door sedan. S.L.Savidge had taken it in on trade and felt it was too far gone to bother fixing for re-sale. For $75.00 it became my first car. It barely ran, seats and upholstery were shot, tires were bald and paint was worn; what a great little car and all mine. At least it had never been in a wreck! The nice thing about cars of this age was that they were very basic and easy to work on. Open the hood and there right in plain view is the engine, carburetor, spark plugs, oil filter, starter and generator. I challenge anyone today to find just one of those items on their new car. I did not get to drive my new car as soon as I had hoped, but I was about to acquire a wealth of basic knowledge about engines and how cars are put together that would that serves me well even today as I still do all routine servicing on my cars and trucks.

The big decision was where to start? It was best to get the messy stuff out of the way first. Luckily my father seemed to be friends with everyone on auto row so we first talked to Al Stratton who owned a garage across the street and had plans to be the dealer for the futuristic Tucker car whose production was now on hold till after the war; or as it turned out, forever. Mr. Stratton gave me my own space on the second floor with a hoist so that I could pull out the engine and send it across the street for rebuilding. While waiting for the engine, I sanded down the body and Al had one of his painters spray paint the car aqua. New brake shoes would make the car a little safer as it had old fashion mechanical brakes activated by a steel rod. You never wanted to assume you were going to stop in old Fords and a driver always had to be ready to apply extreme pressure to the brake pedal.

The real challenge was to find four safe tires. During the war, with no new tires available, re-treading was the only option and when skill-fully done would hopefully last for a while. For reasons unknown there was rubber for the re-treads, but no tires. The rubber came in rolls 6 to 8 inches wide and about ¾ inch thick. The old tire was buffed down and a layer of rubber glued on. Balloons the shape of the tire were put inside and inflated to hold the tires shape and the tire was placed in a cast iron heated mold with an engraved tread pattern. They clamped it down, turned on the heat, inflated the balloons and let it vulcanize for an hour. A miracle, it looked just like a new tire. Naturally, my father came up with another friend and I soon had my four "new" tires. We did not have any steel belts around our tires so no matter how good a tire looked they were very prone to flats and blowouts. Also, with no power steering, a front blowout at any speed meant loss of control. Things were finally coming together; new motor, brakes, tires and a paint job. The interior was still the pits, but luckily my father had not run out of friends.

Floyd Dwight and his father ran an auto upholstery shop nearby on 12th avenue. Floyd agreed to help redo the entire interior; he would sew up, I would install after some instruction. To pay for his time and material I agreed to come in and work for him after school. Together we covered the whole dam interior with bright red leatherette, wow! I would have called it my "pimp mobile" if I had known what a pimp was. Floyd must have liked what I did, for I continued to work for him after school for several years. Due to the war we stayed very busy rebuilding and covering aging seats on older cars.

I guess one always has a soft spot for that first car, especially when you've done so much of the repairs yourself. This was also a time when teenage boys were getting more and more into not only fixing up old wrecks but into modifying cars so that they looked sleeker and had more powerful engines. Unlike today, car engines were not very powerful in the 1930's. My Model A had four large cylinders, but only produced about 45 to 50 H.P... The favorite teen car was a Ford V8 which had about 85 HP. Today I have a four cylinder turbo charged engine that produces 170HP; some difference!

Because of their simplicity these engines were easily modified. The boys put on dual exhausts and carburetors, special manifolds and heads to raise the engines compression ratio. Just like today there always seemed to be interest in going just a little faster. My little "A" was not exactly the best car for "hopping up", but I did find an aluminum "Ray-day" flat head and used it for a while, but found it too hard on the motor. It must have doubled my compression ratio, but since the "A" did not have pressurized oiling the rod bearings would soon knock and required filing down every two to three days. Even though I could now zoom up Capitol Hill in high gear, it was hardly worth the trouble. Next I did away with the muffler and replaced it with a straight pipe right from the manifold. Not a great idea as everyone could hear me coming from a mile away. After numerous calls from the neighbors I put back a smaller muffler. I think I spent more time under the car than in it. It was the easiest car I ever would work on, but it never stopped running or left me miles from home and it did not burn much gas. If I had kept it, or any one of my other cars, they would have been worth much more today than the fancy car I now drive. There came the day when my father sold my "A" for $400 to a man desperate to drive to Denver. That was the start of a long string of cars that the agency did not want and that I would own for a short time, fixing them up so that dad could resell them. On the plus side, after each sale the next car would usually be just a little better.

There came a series of cars, some so-so, some better, and one really bad. My next car was a very nice Model A coupe, all original, but not too good for double dates. As I did not want to keep it I just left it the way it was. Then a very clean 1934 Found Coupe with doors that open forward like in Europe. Ditto, too small. Next a 1937 Chevy two door sedan, my only non Ford car. It ran okay, but the front shocks were worn out so that every time I stopped or started up the front of the car bounced up and down. Rather comical, but distracting.

My worst car ever came as a 1935 Ford four door. That year still had those stupid worn out mechanical brakes which were impossible to get parts for so I had to plan a block ahead if I intended to stop. Every door and window leaked so that the car always smelled like blue cheese, especially bad when one lives in Seattle. Then every so often when shifting the whole leaver would pull right out of the floor and create a slight panic with any passengers. One night after a Noble's Club meeting at my home we went to take some boys home and the car would not start. Everyone pushed and then jump on the running boards as I drove to the service station. Unfortunately, it had escaped me that Gordy, a boy born with only half arms, was seated on the trunk. He had no way to grasp on to the car when I took a corner and fell to the street injuring his head. That car had bad memories and I was happy to see it go, though I felt sorry for whom ever dad sold it to. I temporarily had several cars before settling on a nice 1937 Ford Coupe. I kept this car through the remainder of high school and only put in dual exhausts and super upholstery. It seems I sold it just in time, for the new buyer had the brakes (which I had installed) give out on a steep part of Madison Street and he crashed into a car at a bottom cross street. I think I see that guardian angel again! Although it was my favorite car, while driving it, I was apprehended one time when I laid rubber right in front of a Police car and twice for speeding. This led to a serious discussion with a traffic judge and a sixty day suspension of my driver's license. Sixty days without my car is like forever; I would rather have had a paddle to my butt.

As I look back I realize now how lucky I or any kid in the 1940's was to have his own car. They were hard to find, people did not have much extra money and most kids had to do their own repairs and have a job to pay for gas. I probably took a lot for granted because of my father's job and I also missed a lot in school due to working, but I do feel I had a great time during high school. One thing that was made possible by owning a car was almost nightly visits to the XXX Drive In on Olive way, close to down town. This is where the car lovers and the car modifiers congregated in the evening after dark. This also was one of the few places in Seattle that served good hamburgers, French fries, milk shakes and great root beer. It was not all about food, but was a place to compare cars and show off what you had done. Also, if you thought your car was faster, it was a place to issue a challenge, not unlike what we would see in the movie Grease years later. The races were mostly held late at night on Dexter Avenue; a straight long street that led out to the Fremont Bridge and was used very little at night after Aurora Avenue and the bridge were finished. When the Lake Washington Floating Bridge was built connecting Seattle to Mercer Island it opened up another long straightaway that was seldom patrolled. This run was a little more challenging for 2/3rds of the way across the bridge the highway bulged so that a section could slide out of the way to allow larger ships to pass. As cars approached the bulge at high speed it became a game of chicken as one of the racers had to give way around the curves. After any race everyone was back to the XXX to establish bragging rights.

There were two cars every kid would have given his eye teeth for; a 1936 Ford convertible or 1936 Ford three window coupe. They were both scarce even in those days. It was common to lower the top and windshield and make the cars even sleeker looking; hence the term "chop top". The best 36 convertible belonged to Peter K. from Queen Anne High; bright red with a chopped soft top. It helped that his father was an MD, but I do believe his father liked driving it as much as Peter. Peter was a great athlete and later skated with his sister in the Olympic Pairs competition. I am sure we were all a little jealous.

The name for a car became "a rod" and if it was modified or hopped up it became a "hot rod". I was in more of a fringe area when it came to working on cars as most of my cars stayed fairly stock. My neighbor Remi was very mechanically inclined and loved working on and restoring car engines. He helped build engines for several race cars that ran on the track near Playland on Aurora Ave. and other tracks around the northwest. Another neighbor, Joe D. started a craze for modifying Model A roadsters when he once returned from a visit to California with the first Model "A" roadster with a Ford V8 engine to be seen in this area. That car started a fad, for here was a light car body with no fenders, either a cloth top or no top and an 85 HP engine. It was quicker and faster than any stock car and every teenager and most adults would have loved to have had one. It wasn't long before there were a bunch of these "A-V 8's" on the streets and the city was forced to clamp down on them to make sure they were street legal. I liked attending both stock car and midget races at the Aurora track. I even drove all the way to Portland once to see Remi's car race, but that was as far as my interest in racing ever went.

Having full time access to a car was the determining factor in what I did all during high school and even on through college. The car allowed me and my friends to attend dances and date girls in all parts of the city. During the summer time I would drive almost every weekend to private picnic parks like Shady Beach or Lake Wilderness. I was guilty of having many different girl friends and except for twice, never indulged in anything other than kissing and petting. I always felt I was "with the girl that I loved and loved the girl I was with". Dolly from Lincoln High was small slender girl that was the best dance partner I would ever have. She pressed herself against me and conformed to my every curve. She was so passionate and I was so fond of her that I often wrote her poems. I was fond of Ann for she taught me the proper way to kiss and seemed to enjoy doing it. Carol from Queen Anne was rather a dreamy girl, always with a distant look in her eyes. Very willowy and clinging when we danced. I'll always remember a new years eve when she and I ended up dreamily dancing the night away at the old Trianon Ballroom. Madeline, also from Queen Anne, was as tall as I was and much more mature. She was a woman while I was still being a boy. I went with her to both hers and my proms. I was with her at a program dance at Beaver Lake when a Ballard kid, stag and drunk, wanted to beat the crap out of me because I had been dating his love, Dolly. I probably went out with Sylvia from Lincoln more than any other girl during high school. She also lived the farthest from my home; all the way to 125th north just off Greenwood Avenue. In those days that was a long distance to go for a date, but always well worth the trip. She was tall, blonde and we seemed to always have a great time together. We spent a lot of time at Lake Wilderness swimming, skating, and bowling and scooting down that great water slide. Since she lived just a few blocks from the old Playland we would end many of our dates with a few rides on the Big Dipper. My memories of dating in High school are clear and positive. A boys' biggest problem was lipstick, for it had yet to become "kiss proof" and was forever on every shirt collar and my face. I never left home without a handkerchief and still wonder what my mother thought when she did the wash. I never ceased going with a girl because of an argument; parting was always mutual and friendly. I like the song "I move on" from the musical Chicago; music by John Kander, lyrics by Fred Ebb:

"While trucking down the road of life, although all hope seems gone, I just move on, I move on. When I can't find a single star to hang my wish upon, I just move on, I move on".

Gas rationing limited each auto to five gallons a week so it became a constant battle to find enough fuel to drive to school, go on dates and to places like Shady Beach. Palin's "soccer mom" would have used that up in about five minutes. At times my dad would find an extra B coupon at work and I think it was good for ten or fifteen gallons. My mother only drove a little so often did not use all her coupons and on rare occasions a friend would bum one off their parents. Also George did get the use of his dad's car at times. Siphoning gas was common during the early part of the war, but then they came out with the locking gas cap and ruined one of our sources. Siphoning was really the last resort of a desperate teenager. One almost always had to do it exposed on the street and it was impossible not to get a mouthful of gas along with bad breath. Also, if the police caught you they made it into a big deal.

My friend and neighbor, Remi, parked his car out of sight in a little garage on our alley two doors from his house. I had a date one night, was flat out of gas and had gone through all my usual sources to no avail. I snuck into his garage, loosened a screw in plug to the gas tank and drained a few quarts when in walks Remi. It's dark so he doesn't see me and fires up the car. I was having one of my rare pangs of conscience but finally just had to speak up. I had to replace the plug for I could not let him drive down the alley trailing a stream of gas and then have the car stall. Remi luckily was not a violent type and even allowed me to keep the gas. We also remained friends for many years.

It would be hard to overestimate the effect that cars had on my life from High school on up to the present. They become such an integral and important part of our existence that we tend to take them for granted. What is really amazing is the rapid change in technology since the end of WWII, only a mere sixty years. The car I now drive is like sitting in the cockpit of a 747 Jet compared to my first Model A, yet it still does the same thing; gets me from point A to point B., but in a lot more comfort. We all like to feel we are in control of our own destiny, but in reality its events, often small and inconsequential, that determine our future. I like what Douglas Adams said in "A Hitchhikers Guide to the Galaxy."

"I may not have gone where I intended to go, but I think I have ended up where I intended to be."

6-45: Allies divide Germany and Berlin into zones for occupation; start of cold war.

8-6-45: United States under Truman drops first A Bomb on Hiroshima

8-9-45: Second A Bomb dropped on Nagasaki.

9-2-45: U.S. accepts formal Japanese unconditional surrender on Battleship Missouri.

CHAPTER 14
THE AVALON AND SHADY BEACH

Seems like old times having you to talk with, seems like old times having you to walk with. And it's still a thrill just to have my arms about you, still the thrill that it was the day I found you.

—Carmen Lombardo & John Lorb

S hady Beach is located on the east side of Lake Washington, a few miles north of the town of Kirkland. It was nestled in Juanita Bay facing south so as to receive a full day of sun in summers. There were actually two beaches side by side separated by a hedge and the remains of a wire fence, the other being Juanita Beach. They were both privately owned and operated and almost identical in nature. Each beach may have had 600 to 700 feet of lake frontage and extended several hundred feet deep from the access road, Juanita Drive. The two properties with a total of approximately thirty acres had been settled and developed during the 1920's into resorts by two families; Shady Beach by the D'Alessandro's and Juanita beach by the Forbes who also had their residence on property that was north of Juanita drive. During the years I went to Shady Beach I never realized that both were full scale resorts that also rented cabins as these facilities were on the north side of Juanita drive while I was only interested in the beach and dance hall on the south side. In 1950 all of the property was acquired by King County and later passed to the city of Kirkland. The dance halls are gone along with the great water slide, but it's still a park for picnicking, swimming and walking.

There was an entry fee for a car and driver and an additional charge for passengers that we often sequestered in my car trunk during desperate times even though the entry fee was small. There were full picnic facilities; tables, water and fire pits. Each beach had a long pier, a diving tower; peddle boat rentals and an open air dance hall with a free nickelodeon. We had to pay extra to use the dance hall as I remember being stamped on the hand to enable us to come and go when we needed to eat or take a swim. I do not remember there being a restaurant, but they did sell hamburgers and hot dogs. You could tell that both beaches had been around for a long time as all facilities were well worn. The trees were huge and kept the eating areas well shaded. The Seattle teens that liked to Avalon only came on Sundays and for many years before I started had shown a preference for the Shady beach side. I would go to the other lakes on other days but Sundays were reserved for Shady. It's hard to say how the tradition started or by what group, but I know it existed ten years or more before I started and could have been a popular beach with both teens and adults even before they were doing the Avalon. I feel they chose this beach over other small lakes that also had dance halls because it was the easiest to get to, especially from North Seattle where there was the most interest in the Avalon and teen dancing. The boy's social club such as the Ambassadors and Barons had actually started in North Seattle as dance clubs.

A teenager could get to Shady by driving around the North end of Lake Washington through Bothell then follow Juanita drive along the lake shore to Shady. Also, there was the ferry from the foot of Madison Street that went to Kirkland leaving only a few miles north to Shady. Teens from the Montlake and Madison districts were more liable to use the ferry so as to save on gas. Also, in the 1930's there was still a fleet of passenger Mosquito boats operating on the Lake so one did not even need a car. I knew very few kids who drove their own cars, but most had occasional use of the family car and would take turns driving to Shady. There was a lot of sharing of rides and even though cars were scarce during the depression years the teens still managed somehow to make it to Shady on Sunday. It was often easier to get to Shady than to find a way back home. On occasion a person's ride would have to leave early or the boy wanted privacy with a new girl he had met and his riders would be left to fend for themselves. Several times when I did not come in my own car I would snag a ride with what seemed to be the last car out of Dodge. Then I would get dumped in the general vicinity of home and have to hoof it the remainder of the way. I remember one time I had driven to Shady in a 1939 Plymouth Sedan that my father borrowed from his agency. We usually went home when it started to get dark for we always wanted to be bright and cheerful for school on Monday. That night there seemed to be an unusual number of kids that needed a ride back to Seattle so I kept saying okay till there were a total of thirteen of us crammed into my car. I drove back through Bellevue so as to cross the new floating bridge. At this time there was no highway 405 and no fancy interchange access leading to Mercer Island. The road as it approached I-90 was slightly down hill and then turned sharply left for Mercer Island or right to go under the highway and to Issaquah. I found that as I approached the access I had such a load that my brakes would not slow me and I was afraid that if I tried to turn to sharply the weight would cause the car to roll. Best choice was straight ahead into a ditch, but slowly. Not all my passengers thought I had made the correct decision and most were ready to walk the rest of the way home. We lucked out as a man with a truck and tow chain came by to help. There was a lot of grumbling and snide comments aimed at my driving skills, but everyone finally got back in as it was still a long way to Seattle; it was my driving skills versus a long walk. The bottom of the front grill was bent back a little and did not go unnoticed by the S.L. Savidge manager. He sent out a stern warning that salesman's kids were no longer to drive company cars. Bummer!!

I think the reason for increased interest from north end teens was that it was just a lot easier and more convenient for them to drive to Shady. The majority of teens I met came from Ballard, Roosevelt and Lincoln with a few from Franklin and Garfield. I am sure this changed over the years as the beaches popularity increased.

Why had teens originally chosen Shady over Juanita? I feel that the big reason was that the management at Shady catered to those kids that liked to Avalon. The dance floor was always in good shape, they supplied powdered wax to keep the floor slippery and mainly they always had the latest songs that we loved to dance to in their free nickelodeon. The second big reason was that Shady had this killer water slide that used a board on wheels to skim you over the water. This was a one of a kind slide, never seen before or since. First you rented a four foot long by eighteen inch wide board with four small wheels on the bottom. The slide structure was right alongside the pier and seemed about fifty feet high when you were climbing up, but was probably more like thirty. You placed the wheels inside an L shaped metal track, laid on the board, crossed your fingers and shoved off. The first portion dropped steeply to help gain speed and as one approached the water the slide leveled out and shot you skimming out over the water for up to twenty or thirty feet. I am sure any thinking adult would have given second thoughts before going on this rickety contraption, but danger was never a consideration, in fact, on most rides we went double or even triple, like teenage pancakes, so as to share the price of a board rental. I never heard of anyone being injured which is a good thing because I do not believe places like this were big on insurance, but then people in the 40's were not into suing like we are today and were more likely to assume responsibility for their own screw-ups. I loved that slide and felt that which does not kill me only postpones the inevitable.

The country surrounding Seattle was full of picnic areas open only in the summer, although a few opened the dance halls in the winter for special group dances. Many like Beaver, Angle, Echo and Wilderness were located on lakes of the same name and also had dance halls and amenities similar to Shady. Echo Lake was just a little north of the Seattle city limits which at that time was North 65th. Angle Lake was in the South end, but catered to a more adult drinking crowd. The dance hall at Indianola was even popular in my father's time, but closed when the land was sub-divided and became private. When we now attempt to drive on the East side of Lake Washington it's hard to imagine that this area was ever sparsely populated as it has become one of Washington's largest cities. When I went to Shady Beach or Lake Wilderness it was a drive in the country; no homes, a few farms, trees and narrow roads.

The city of Bellevue was made up of only three or four blocks on Main Street and Kirkland was a small town clustered around the ferry dock.

Going to Shady was a full day plus a little more. I would usually pick up friends on the way, but always came home with more than I took. When I first started to go to Shady it was on the Ferry to Kirkland, but later we always seemed to drive. It may have been that they raised the ferry fare or that each car passenger had to pay, so with a full car load it cost less to drive. For me It was about the same distance to go North through Bothell as it was to take the new floating bridge that had been finished in 1940. With the removal of the toll the bridge became the best route from Montlake.

I was working so I know I always had some money, but since we went to so many dances and drove so much I was generally short of cash. I packed a lot of lunches and if I took a date I could usually talk her into bringing food. Occasionally we would buy a burger, but even though fifty cents seems so little today it meant over two gallons of gas then. Since there was a non-fence between Shady and Juanita we crossed over often just to check it out. If some group was having a big picnic with twenty or thirty people we would just join the group and blend in. With large picnics no one knew everyone and usually half the people were coming and going to the beach leaving all that food just sitting lonely on the tables. If it hadn't been for us it probably would have spoiled. The days seemed to go by so fast. We swam, we danced then swam some more or rented a board for the slide, danced some more, stole a little food, swam and dove off the tower and usually finished the evening dancing. By then I was getting hungry, was out of money and knew I had to head for home if I wanted to be fed.

I have to comment again on just how unusual was this dance we called the Avalon. First it should be noted that teenagers five to ten years earlier called the dance the "Grapevine". I can understand that name as a large part of the dance was weaving to the side and back again. One friend of mine thought it might have come from the resort and dance hall on Catalina Island called Avalon. It's been so long that the origins are hard to trace. In Seattle teenagers started doing the Grapevine sometime during the thirties and continued doing the Avalon until the end of the Big Band era, maybe through the fifties. It started in North Seattle and was aided by dance oriented social clubs like Barons, Nobles and Ambassadors. When I started going to dances the Avalon was much more popular in the north end schools, but in talking to graduates of the 50's it had later become very popular in all the schools.

Also, unlike today, during the school year there were dances and dance halls everywhere; the PTAs held weekly dances at the Ballard, Franklin and West Seattle Field Houses. Roosevelt and Lincoln combined to hold dances at the Green lake Field house. Then there were also the very popular Margret Tapping and the Mount Baker community center. On any weekend there would be one or two dances somewhere on both Friday and Saturday nights. Once a year we looked forward to the All City PTA dance held at the Civic Auditorium. It was open to all teens and they even hired a name band. When the PTA dances ceased in the summer the slack was taken up by the opening of the picnic areas and dance halls at the nearby lakes. A teenager was never without a place to dance. And mainly the soft sentimental music from the big bands was a perfect match for the flowing movements of the Avalon.

What more could a teenage couple ask for in a dance. The boy gets to hold the girl, who is pressing her cashmere clad body against him for the entire dance. The floor is slick with wax and the couples take long sliding steps without ever separating. The boy "grapevines" out to the side, but the girl stays firm against him, next he makes a graceful turn and slides backwards for a few steps, but never losing the girl with her head nestled against his chest. A few long slides, another turn and the boy again faces forward, the girl always pressed against him, never missing a step, you are sure the two are literally glued together. To watch a really good couple dance, like my friends Gene and Maxine M., is like a symphony in motion. When we have such great dancers and the dance is almost like an art form, it is only natural to want to know who the best is. At program dances and the All City they held tag dance contests. The band would always play Hoagy Carmichael's Stardust as that was the perfect song for doing the Avalon:

> Sometimes I wonder why I spend the lonely night dreaming of a song? The melody haunts my reverie and I am once again with you, when our love was new and each kiss an inspiration.
> —M. Parish & Hoagy Carmicheal

Then everyone would dance. Four of five judges on stage would select ten or twelve dancers whom they felt were the best and everyone else would clear the floor while those picked continued to dance. The judges then pick three of the best dancers who would dance a little more and then came up on the stage. The crowd applauded for the one they liked best and prizes were awarded. At an all city dance five years before my time, my friend's brother Bob M. and his partner Betty H., both from Ballard, had won first place. To me who had only been tagged once it was like winning the Super Bowl.

A few words about fast dancing or what we call the "Jitterbug" and what others in Europe called "Swing Dancing". I feel that this type of dancing was more popular in the 1930's, but was seen less after the war started and the songs became mostly slower and more sentimental which lent themselves to the Avalon. In looking through many songs written after 1941 only a few were swing tunes, such as Tuxedo Junction, Juke Box Saturday Night, One O'clock Jump, G.I. Jive and Tiger Rag. When a fast song was played only a few would dance while all the others just gathered around to watch. One boy, Wes, from Ballard was a standout doing the Jitterbug and he always seemed to be able to find a good partner. He could even do the splits and bounce back up to standing. After watching him the rest of us were probably too intimidated and self conscious to even try. Mostly, swing dancing was popularized in the movies as a show stopper.

In my dad's time the men wore shirt and tie, slacks and sport coats. With every generation the dress code deteriorated a little till lately boys wear oversized pants around their butts and weird T-shirts all winter long and no coats. I suppose all teens have a dress code designed to express individuality, but mainly to irritate their parents. Except for my dirty white cords my dress was pretty sharp compared to today's teens. My standard was a candy stripe small collar dress shirt worn under a Lord Jeff V neck sweater. The shirt was held tight around the neck by a rubber band wrapped around a low shirt button and then to the top pants button. I would have preferred a cashmere sweater, but they were still too expensive. By the time I had finished high school I owned only one. Shoes were all leather, pebble grain by Nun Bush. Before wearing a new pair I would take them to the cobbler and have small metal plates inset into both the heel and the toe to help cut down on wear. That helped, but since I wore the shoes to school and for dancing they wore rapidly in the center and would have to be re-soled, but that could be done only one time.

My hair was very blonde and light weight so was always a problem to care for. At first it was regular with a part, then a crew cut followed by a crew cut with long sides and a ducktail in back. I finally settled on a straight crew cut which I stayed with forever. Not every barber was able to give the perfect crew cut which had to be ruler flat on top and I would travel miles to visit that barber with the right touch. I spent many hours with a brush trying to convince my hair to grow up rather than flat. My jacket was a letterman's style, but never with a letter. I think my dirty cords and that ducktail were my parent's only complaint. I had to watch my mother because she was always trying to grab my cords to wash them especially after I had worked on my car. They did allow me a charge account at Nordstrom's as long as I was not excessive.

The girls that attended our dances had their own dress code which all boys loved. They wore very tight long skirts that accentuated the girls butt. They had slits in the side so the girl could still take those long steps when dancing. The best part was that they all seemed to be able to afford cashmere or Angora sweaters which made them extremely soft and cuddly when dancing and also after dancing. They had their white leather shoes with a wedged sole call Joyce's. Almost all girls wore their hair shoulder length and I don't remember anyone changing the color. Girls that did not attend many dances seemed to stay with pleated skirts; Yuk!

We went to so many dances that it was only natural to assume that the Avalon was wide spread and everyone was doing it. Nothing was farther from the truth. Even at my school Garfield, it was only in my last year of school that some of the kids started to try dancing the Avalon. In my first year of college at Eastern Washington I never saw one person dance the Avalon and I never had a date or attended a dance. My second year I came back home to attend the University and also joined a fraternity. Same thing, no one from out of Seattle and very few that lived in Seattle knew anything about this dance. I had to ask my old high school girl friends to attend our functions so that I had someone to dance with. Again, after my first year at the University I drove to New York to see my first girl friend Lilly Jean. The local girls had no Idea what dance I was trying to do, but then they had never heard of the hamburger or the milkshake and I got tired of trying to explain them. In defense of New Yorkers, I did have my first Pizza there years ahead of Pizza Pete.

So by the late 1950' things were starting to change. Les Paul invented that infernal solid body electric guitar. Elvis learned to play it and started to gyrate and jazz up his songs. Then Ed Sullivan brought over the Beatles and it was like the flood gates opened. Then came the Rolling Stones, Led Zeppelin, Kiss and on and on till they blew those gentle big bands right off the stage. Suddenly music became a spectator sport with broken ear drums and no dancing as we had once known it. Most of the dance halls across the country closed. In Seattle you can still get a dance at the Elks clubs. I did hear a program the other day on PBS about a man who is restoring a few of the thousands of old dance halls in Texas. So, maybe there's still a heartbeat left.

9-45: By the end of the war, all Japanese vessels at Pearl Harbor had been sunk.

10-24-45: The United Nations is re-born.

11-45: The Nuremberg trials for Nazi war criminals begin.

CHAPTER 15
THE BIG BANDS
AND THE ERA OF SWING

I fall in love to easily, I fall in love fast, I fall love to terrible
hard for love to ever last.

—J. Styne & S. Cahn.
—Sung by Sinatra in the movie "Anchors Away"

I do not remember showing any interest in Big Band music before
I started going to dances and learning to do the Avalon. Neither I nor
any of my friends had much access to music. I would not have a record
player till I was at least sixteen and then it was an extremely basic unit
with a tiny built in speaker. Our only radio was that large cabinet in the
living room which was very seldom on except for serials right before
dinner and Sunday comedies after our main meal. There were very few
radios small enough to be on the kitchen counter and once the war
started there were no new radios of any kind available. Things like the
Walkman or the I Pod were not even a glimmer in our imagination. It's
hard for someone today to even imagine a car coming without a radio,
CD player and eight speakers. My first three or four cars did not have
radios or even a place to put one, nor did they have heaters which, when
winter arrived, I felt was more important than any radio. When I finally

acquired a car with both a heater and a built in radio I felt things would never get better than this even though the reception stopped several miles out of town; but the heater still worked.

Then, as I started to attend dances, I felt a revelation that music transported me and put me in a special mood. Dancing the Avalon to this new found soft gentle music doubled my pleasure. Suddenly I started to notice that the Big Band music was being played everywhere. Many restaurants installed large nickelodeons, often with a song selector in each booth; and it stayed a nickel a song for many years. I bought my first record player (windup) and shortly afterwards purchased my second which had a motor and a tiny speaker. How could things possible get any better? I then started to collect a few records, all 78 RPM and 10 inches in diameter. Over those years I may have purchased at most forty records. So that amounts to maybe eighty songs, one on each side. Today I have a stack of CD's and each one has up to fifteen songs, most of which you put up with just to listen to that song you like.

Often, when not working, we took the bus downtown after school to visit a record store on Fifth near the Fifth Avenue Theater. It was the only place I can remember that sold records, though there probably were others. Each record came in its own unsealed paper envelope and one could take the record into a tiny booth and listen to the whole thing; which was only three minutes. Each record would have a major band or artist on side A and a lesser artist on side B. It was not necessary to buy ten songs just to get one you liked. We could play records all afternoon and then return them to the desk where the clerk would thank you for listening and even smile. I believe a single record cost about one dollar, but we bought very few because we were always going to dances where we could hear the songs on a good Whirlitzer player for free.

Because bands would record only one song at a time they produced records more frequently and we could pick and choose as a new recording would be along next week. Also to consider is that big bands seldom played their own music. Music was written by professionals in what became known as "tin pan alley". The music business had concentrated in an area on Broadway in New York between 42nd and 50th streets. The name, "tin pan", came not from the street, but from the sound of pianos furiously pounded by "song pluggers" demonstrating tunes to publishers. Some big name writers were Sammy Cahn, Julie Styne, Johnny Mercer, Hoagy Carmichael, Bud Green, Harry Warren, Maxwell Anderson, M. Parish and on and on. Last but not least were the songs from Broadway shows written by the Gershwin's, Rogers and Heart and Cole Porter. It was nice that their best songs would come out as singles often sung by big names like Frank Sinatra and you only had to buy the one song you liked not a whole album! The difference today is that rock groups tend to write and play mainly their own songs; written often by various members of the group. It may take one or two years for a group to come up with enough songs for a new album. Another big difference is that there are now thousands of groups making recordings so the choices become mind boggling.

The big bands that we listened and danced to in the 40's had their start back in the mid-20's. Some early big names were Paul Whitman, Rudy Vallee, Guy Lombardo, Vincent Lopez and Fred Waring. The groups could be from ten to twenty pieces, the music was a sweeter form of jazz, but rather highly arranged with very little improvisation. They also usually included violins which were dropped with the introduction of swing around 1935. What we came to know in the 40's was a fusion of styles from various parts of the country as well as from various ethnic groups.

Swing developed from three major centers; New York, Chicago and Kansas City. Over time better musicians from all over would migrate to these centers. Count Basie was in Kansas City; Louis Armstrong brought that feel of Dixieland jazz to Chicago from New Orleans and along with him came trombonist Jack Teagarden, drummer Gene Krupa and clarinetist Benny Goodman. The Afro-American influence was strong in New York for besides Louis Armstrong there was Duke Ellington, Billy Holliday, Cab Callaway and Fats Waller. These men were extremely talented musicians and loved to get together and play their form of jazz in after hour's jam sessions. This brought about a change in the format of jazz so that soon the emphasis was placed more on talented individuals in a band which in turn led to each section of the band being given a chance for a solo "riff". Along with this the rhythmic beat was smoothed out so that it was not as jumpy as with Vallee or

Lombardo, typified by dances like the Lindy Hop. Then finally there was the influence of both music and dance from Latin America; the Tango from Argentina, the Rumba from Cuba and especially the Bossa Nova from Brazil, made famous by Stan Getzs' "The Girl from Ipanema". The resulting mix of music was wildly popular through two decades, extending through the 1940's and 50's and was played by literally thousands of bands across the country.

The single most important influence in jazz was Louis Armstrong. Born in New Orleans in 1901 to a poor family he never finished grade school. He picked up an interest in music while in a reform school. He was self taught never having any formal training. He played all over the world, but found less discrimination in Europe. He was a champion of the Negro cause and even wrote to President Eisenhower to take action against Governor Faubus of Arkansas for not allowing Black children to attend Little Rock Central High School. He loved all sorts of music from the Beatles to Opera. Everyone should listen to his rendition of, "It's a Wonderful World."

Seattle had its share of small bands of from eight to ten members from high school age on up. They played for the Nobles and Barons high school program dances, for all the small dance halls in and around Seattle, but usually only once or twice a week. Some big halls like the Trianon or Parkers might keep a band going for weeks. The really big names like Duke Ellington, Benny Goodman or the Dorsey brothers toured a great deal, but the majority of bands were regional and played only the lesser dance halls.

When those big name bands did come to Seattle it was a major event and they would either play in one of the large downtown theaters or at the Civic Auditorium. It was only natural that we would try to see them just like later teens flocked to see Presley or the Beetles. I never could afford to buy a ticket, but one weekend when Tommy Dorsey was to play at the Civic three of us decided to just go down and hang out with the crowd; maybe sneaking in was in the back of our minds. As we milled around outside we noticed this one place where the chain link fence around the storage sheds came right next to the storage roof which in turn butted up against the Auditorium wall. What the hell, we got up on the shed roof and then spied a ladder fastened to the side of the Auditorium that led clear to the roof, maybe up another fifty feet. The climb was becoming a little scary and I was really feeling those butterflies in my stomach. Best to just hang on tight to those rungs and don't look down. On the roof top was a large hatch which we managed to pry open and could then look straight down on a cat walk and further to the stage where the band was playing. Now it was a long, long way down and the butter flies were taking over, but it was no time to chicken out so we climbed over the edge and down a ladder to the first cat walk and just watched. That was good enough, for continuing down to the stage was not an option. Eventually we climbed back out keeping a death grip on the rungs; replaced the hatch and made our way home with memories of a great adventure. The ground never felt so good. I hate those butterflies and never have and never will get used to heights.

This was music that people loved to dance to and its popularity spread with the aid of remote radio broadcasts that had been newly initiated by the major networks. So now people at home could listen to their favorite big bands as they played in ballrooms and clubs across the country. Immense dance halls like the Savoy and Roseland in New York, the Grand Valley Dale in Columbus, Ohio and the Palomar in Los Angeles drew huge crowds and the biggest name bands, but almost every town in America had a dance hall. Seattle had the Trianon Ballroom located just north of downtown and Parkers located farther north on Aurora in what was our old roller rink. Some broadcasts came from night clubs such as the Cotton Club and the Coconut Grove. It was radio that really spread the interest in big bands and it seemed like we could tune in at almost any time and hear swing music. The other big thing that helped popularize big bands was the introduction of the nickelodeon. It became common even in the smallest eating place to have a Wurlitzer sitting in the corner and at a nickel a song they were always playing. This raging popularity of the big bands continued during the war and through the 40's, started a slow decline during the 50's as the music began reflecting the influence from bebop, art music, cool jazz and pop rock. This change was slower to hit the high schools where the interest in big band music and dancing the Avalon grew stronger and wider spread in the Seattle area during the 50's.

The big name bands toured just like the bands of today and the fans lined up hours ahead of time yelling and screaming when their favorites showed up. That's where the similarity ceases. The bands and singers were much more approachable and not protected by dozens of burly security guards blaring out warnings over hand held speakers. Inside there were no twenty foot high stacks of speakers ready to tear at your ear drums, but just the volume that twenty or so instruments of the band could generate. Because there were no gimmicks used on stage or in making a record a band would sound exactly the same in person as on a record; there was no dubbing in, reverb chambers or other electronic gadgets to cloud a personal message from that special performer that you loved.

The one electronic gadget that came along about 1935 and made a big difference in how vocalists approached singing was the stage microphone. This usually was the only part of the band that was amped. It ushered in the day of the star vocalist such as; Ella Fitzgerald, Billie Holiday, Helen Forest, Peggy Lee, Doris Day, Jo Stafford and of course the best known and most popular singer of our era, Frank Sinatra. Sinatra was born in Hoboken, New Jersey in 1915 and began his singing career as a member of the Hoboken Four who took first prize on the Major Bowles Amateur Hour. His first night club gig was as a singing waiter. In 1939 he joined the Harry James band and made his first recording; "All or Nothing at All". In 1940 he joined the Tommy Dorsey band and recorded his first major hit: "I'll Never Smile Again", a song typical for those times as it told of the yearning and despair of a generation being torn apart by war. These were songs familiar to all age groups unlike today where songs are written for teens and seldom about the effects of war. Also, you never heard swear words or sexual innuendo's in any song. In 1941 Sinatra was voted the Outstanding Male Vocalist and in December of 42 he made his first solo recording; "Night and Day" and appeared with Benny Goodman at the Paramount Theater in New York as an "extra added attraction". No one up till now had realized just how much his popularity had spread, for when he was introduced on stage there was a mass hysteria that created headlines across the country. The era of the Bobby Soxer had begun and hysterical scenes would be repeated wherever Frank sang. He sang on the Hit Parade radio show from 1943 to 45 which was just the start of a long and tumultuous career. He was a friend of both Mafia members and John Kennedy. He headlined in Las Vegas, owned a part of the Sands and starred in movies. Hoover of the FBI tracked him and felt he was a communist, but came to his aid when Frank's son was kidnapped in 1963. He was head of the "Rat Pack" and chairman of the board. He was important in my time for he took songs written by others and sang them in a way that made them very urgent and personal; everyone related to and felt a special sensation when he sang. He had a soft, effortless voice that captivated teenagers and as Sinatra once said, "When I sing, I believe, I'm honest."

These bands played a big part in lifting our troop's moral during the war. They toured with the USO troops throughout the European and Pacific theaters. Many big stars enlisted in the service and toured with the USO at the fronts, the most notable being Glenn Miller whose plane was shot down on the eve of the Battle of the Bulge while crossing the English Channel. He was one of our super stars with such hits as; "Moonlight Serenade", "A String of Pearls", "Chattanooga Choo Choo" and "Stardust", most of which are still being played today. We recently lost another of my era's big singing stars, Joe Stafford who was in my mind the female version of Sinatra. She grew up during the depression studying classical music. She sang with the Pied Pipers and the Tommy Dorsey band and in 1944 went solo. She was extremely popular especially with the GI's and would sell over 25 million records; a lot for any time. In the 50's she had a very popular television show. She died at the age of 90.

Now we may think that with the entry of the Beatles, Elvis, The Stones and a zillion other rock bands this would sound a death knoll for the gentle music of the Big Bands. Wrong, there are still people who like to dance and listen to music while still retaining their hearing. The real surprise for me came recently from of all places, Rod Stewart, one of the world's top rockers. It turns out he has been warming up to do his concerts for years by singing our old favorites like, "The Way You Look Tonight," "These Foolish Things," and "You go to my Head." In 2002 he put together an album of songs that anyone of my generation would love. It turns out he already knew the words to 2/3rds of the songs. He even put up his own money for the first album. There must be a lot of music lovers like me left, for he has now finished four albums of the songs that my generation danced to in high school. As Bill Zehme said, "The bounty of all you will hear, I can only promise, should go to your head and stay in your heart—forever. That's all."

It also turns out that the interest in our old big band music is rapidly increasing in Europe as is the interest in slow dancing. In America we have the only all request "Big Band Broadcast" emanating from New York and narrated by Chris Valenti. It's on every Saturday evening for three hours. It's a request program and the lines are always jammed, so keep dialing. It's new for some and brings back memories for others. They receive a ton of mail thanking them for the show and as one man wrote in, "These songs have passed from hand to hand, bequeathed to us, by America's big bands.

1946: We exchange the hot war for a cold war that would dominate our foreign policy for over the next fifty years.

1948-53: Russia blockades Berlin denying Allies access. U.S. brings in supplies by air.

CHAPTER 16
THE GRADUATE AND
HIGHER EDUCATION

Yesterday all my troubles seemed so far away, now it looks as though they're here to stay, Oh, I believe in yesterday—1965

—The Beatles

It seems strange that so much about my high school years remains so clear except my actual graduation and prom. I am sure I graduated, at least I am fairly sure, but I can't remember that moment when they actually handed the diploma to me. I know I attended two proms; Garfield's and Queen Anne's, but have never been able to recall where they were held and I know this is not from the effects of alcohol. I am sure I borrowed my parent's car so I could double date as my car at that time was a business coupe. I have a fleeting image of me and my date on horseback somewhere out near Woodinville after one of these proms. I guess it's not important what you do on prom night as long as you stay up all night. A few of us decided to ride horses.

The summer of 1946, for me, was to prepare for college, something I had not done enough of in high school. The draft was still in effect, but if a student chose to continue their education they would be granted a temporary deferment and be classified 4A. Even though my grade

My Prom Date

point average was barely 2.2 there was never a doubt in my mind that I would attend college. Not every boy in my graduation class chose that route. Many opted to join the military and satisfy their two year obligation as soon as possible. There was an advantage to joining upon graduation; we were still boys and unsure of what we wanted for a career, they no longer had to serve in battle, but only as occupation troops in Germany or Japan and when through they received a bonus of free tuition and books to the college of their choice. They got to see the world, I got to continue going to Shady Beach.

Those of us who play; pay. With my low grade point I was having a difficult time convincing a college to accept me. My first choice had been the University of Washington, but I was refused admission due to low grades and due to a large influx of returning GI's taking advantage of a free education. I tried several small teachers colleges in Washington and was finally accepted at Eastern Washington College located in Cheney, (no relation to our future Secretary of State) just thirty miles west of Spokane and the Idaho state line. At this time I had very little knowledge of anything east of the Cascade's and would have been perfectly happy to keep it that way. My only excursion east had been to Yakima when my father delivered a car to a hop farmer. My recollections of that trip were the intense smell of ripe hops and large buzzing grasshoppers.

As my time of internment at Cheney drew near it was decided by some higher authority that I would have no need for a car at school, for I was going to immerse myself in campus life and my studies. That day finally arrived when my mother and father drove me to Cheney mid week so that I would have time to "settle in" and sign up for classes. When I arrived in Cheney I was in a state of utter shock; here was this postage sized speck of green campus in the middle of the Sahara. I was about to exchange the green of the west for the arid barrenness of the east. The town, what there was of it, was small, old and run down. It had once been touted as a main railroad terminal, but lost out to Spokane and was immediately forgotten. To compound my problems the nice brick men's dorm was full, also due to the large numbers of returning GI's. To fill in "temporarily" the school had purchased an old Army H barracks which they planted out in the sagebrush a block or so from the campus. The building was prefab wood with leaky wood windows, steam heat at times and nary a sign of insulation. It was my luck to be given a room on what was in winter, "the windward side." The continual strong winds picked up the surrounding top soil blowing it through the cracks on to every surface in my room. Now I understood how those legionnaires felt living at the fort in Beau Guest.

As I registered for classes I received shock number two; being basically a teachers college they did not have a pre-engineering curriculum. This really dampened my spirits which I felt could get no worse, as I was set on being a mechanical engineer. Drat! I had to substitute various math classes for what should have been calculus and there was no mechanical drawing, I would miss the two most important courses in pre-engineering. To get my credits I now had to fill in with whatever course was available, like chemistry which I detested. I knew I was about to flunk chemistry when they handed me that clear vial of liquid and told me to find out its contents. Yeh, like I am from the EPA.

Eastern Washington's failure to have my necessary pre-engineering courses is another example of how small unplanned events tend to determine a person's future course. I was able to enroll the following year at the U of W in engineering. Due to this mix up in my math I was then placed in an advanced calculus class to help me catch up which proved to be way over my head causing me to drop out of engineering. After joining a fraternity my best friend, whose father was an Optometrist, talked me into enrolling with him in Optometry at Pacific University in Forest Grove, Oregon. We don't plan our futures; it's just a crap shot.

At the onset the school, the town of Cheney and the cold climate seemed like an invitation to a disaster. Cheney was a wide spot in the road that time had passed by. There were two small cafes, taverns, gas stations and a grain elevator. The campus had a little greenery, a really tiny swim pool and a student union building. The pool and the student union would be where I would spend most of my spare time and would help me adjust to this "monastic" life. It was difficult for me to keep focused on the idea that I was actually there for an education, but I was aware of one thing, not having a car was starting to bother me. I was beginning to feel like Patrick McGowan in the TV series "The Prisoner."

My parents liked to tell the story about my first week at Cheney. They had dropped me off mid-week then drove to Yakima before returning to Seattle. I had decided that three days in a row was enough so I walked to the I 90 highway which ran through town and thumbed a ride back to Seattle. My parents just barely beat me home. Sunday morning my parents drove me to the other end of the floating bridge where I thumbed a ride back to school. Hitchhiking in 1946 was still an accepted way to travel as new cars were still in short supply. Drivers had become used to giving servicemen and others a ride during the war and this attitude continued for many years.

Hitchhiking was not without its perils. I recall one time when I caught a ride home in an old 1934 Plymouth Sedan. I could see when it stopped that It was rather beat up, but most cars in those days were old and worn looking. But, when I climbed in the back seat I was greeted by an enormous and overly friendly Saint Bernard. I told the couple I was headed to Seattle, but was so busy fighting off the dog that I did not notice when they had turned south off I 90 on to the road to Yakima. They apparently felt all roads led to Seattle. So now it's getting dark and I have been dumped off in Yakima covered in dog hair and slobber and nearly broke. What a way to start a weekend. I located the bus depot as it was getting too late to hitchhike. I was low on money and faced the decision of either buying a bus ticket or food. I was still three hours away from home, but at least I could settle back and maybe catch some shut-eye on the drive. Wrong; the bus turned out to be an old city type bus, cold, drafty and with rock hard one position seats with that iron grip rail across the top. With no way to relax or get comfortable and 150 miles of bad road ahead I am thinking there has to be a car in my future.

Just a few weeks later, when the memory of the dog trip had faded,

I was again thumbing my way to Seattle. A cool looking young guy in a nice convertible stopped to give me a ride. I made sure he was going straight to Seattle and had no animals in the car. I thought this is the way to travel, warm comfortable car and good conversation even though I was aware he was driving a little fast. It turns out the guy had been taking a little nip now and then. Hard to tell how long, but as we approached Snoqualmie pass his driving became more and more erratic. Remember I 90 was still a curvy two lane road and not in great shape. My nervous tension was mounting as he had increasing difficulty staying in his lane. I was having visions of us leaving the highway and me being launched through the canvas roof into the forest, never to be found. I was not a great believer in miracles, but making it to Seattle came close to being one.

I thought it would never happen, but I did start to adjust to campus life. I made a few friends most of whom were older and had been in the service. Why they would befriend an eighteen year old kid from the big city is hard to figure. One boy was a Crow Indian from Montana who drove a large Buick convertible always with the top down; no matter what the temperature. He wore this fleece lined bomber coat while the rest of us froze; but no feather. There was Sketter B., a boy from Camas Washington who was maybe 5'4" tall, but was a terror on roller skates and a great diver off the high tower. As the weather warmed in the spring he taught me a little of the art of diving. We drove in many times to the roller rink in Spokane where he would enter races and perform tricks in the center rink. He would also grab me by a foot and arm and spin me around, a trick I was never too fond of. One couple that befriended me, were always threatening to runoff to Montana to get married as he had been away in the service for some while. They were different than those I may have associated with had I remained in Seattle, but were thoughtful, gentle and easy going.

I spent an increasing amount of time with my new friends at the student union eating club sandwiches and learning to play Eastern Washington Bridge called pinochle. Socially things were looking up a bit, but school was heading the other way. I lost interest as I knew the courses I was taking would not help with engineering. In sports I turned out for the basketball team, but I was nowhere good enough to make the team. At this particular time the two Liefer boys were on the team and could pretty well sink a basket from any location on the court. A few years earlier they had taken a team from a tiny town nearby to the state basketball championship. All the team needed were three other guys to pass them the ball. I spent more time in the pool passing my life-saving and first aid and nearly drowned several times playing water polo. Life was almost bearable, except for this one ex GI in the room directly across the hall from me.

I'll call him Joe and he is taking pre dentistry. We were the only students down this one ground floor hall so became fairly friendly. I received mail regularly from Wilma K. a girl I was dating in Seattle. One day Joe took it on himself to pick up my mail, but went a little too far and opened Wilma's letter and read it. Then, because I was a number of years his junior he decided to tease me about what Wilma had written. A letter from one's girl friend is a serious matter and not to be made light of by some weirdo. Instead of going along with the jest I went a little berserk, grabbed him in a choke hold and made him say uncle. He did not realize that I was rather strong for my size and it caught him off guard. He handed me back the letter, but I knew I was in trouble when he then reaches in a drawer and hauls out a 45 caliber pistol, which he probably stole from the Army, and points it at my head. Having a gun pointed at you causes intense fear and weak knees and possibly dirty underwear. Next to firing the gun it's a quick way to terminate any friendship. I continued to be nervous about having a big gun across the hall so I tried to time my coming and going to avoid him. I am still not sure why I never reported him.

Eastern Washington turns to winter in a big way which I found difficult to adjust to. There was nothing to interrupt the icy winds which seemed never to stop blowing. I promised myself that should I escape from Cheney I would live in a forest where the wind and top soil can't reach me. It was early in the winter that this couple decided they could not wait an instant longer to get married. At the time of this decision we were scarfing down a few beers at the Old Log Inn just across the state line in Idaho. Idaho was one of the first states to conclude that if you're old enough to be shot in some foreign country you are old enough to have a beer before leaving. At this time, the only place to get a quickie marriage was in Superior Montana just a few hundred miles away. No problem, leave now and we'll be there in the morning, get hitched and back that same day. If I had actually had any knowledge of what it took to drive to Superior, especially in the winter, I would have immediately thumbed my way back to Cheney.

Under the influence of alcohol all adventures seem doable. Did it concern us that we were driving an old 1934 Plymouth with a poor heater? NO! Should we worry that the tires have little remaining tread and we have no chains? Not to worry! Let's have another beer. We drove on through Coeur'd' Alene, then on up to Kellogg where the old two lane highway starts to climb and climb and climb into the mountains. I see why they called it Lookout Pass for on a clear day one might be able to see the Pacific Ocean. We were in luck and it did not start to seriously snow till after we had passed the summit. We made it to Superior, holed up in a motel and checked in to the courthouse early the next morning to cement the union. I was more than happy to be heading home, but overnight it had snowed about six inches and the going without traction devices was becoming a little dicey. We started down off the pass toward Kellogg where ice had replaced the snow on our road. It was near impossible to slow the car and stepping on the brakes was to invite disaster. The fact that there were no guard rails heightened my nervousness and I kept a death grip on any nearby solid object. Then it happened, we lost traction completely and the car went into a slow death spiral. I was ready to jump out before we plunged into the bottomless abyss. I think I saw this heaven sent ray of sun strike the car for as the car slowly went backward toward the edge it struck the only snow berm to have built up on the roads outer edge for as far as the eye could see. Was this another intervention aimed at me, or was it aimed at the newlyweds and I just happened to be along?

For the first time I think I was enjoying being back at Cheney. It was nice just to play a little water polo and hang out at the student union playing pinochle and eating BLT's. A week later one of my friends, whose father was a wheat rancher, invited me to his home near Wilber for the weekend. Not exactly Shady Beach, but sounded like fun and would be a nice break. I had a great time; nice parents, good food, but then we decided to attend the weekly Saturday night dance on the second floor of the Grange hall. It reminded me a lot of the time I attended a dance at Burton on Vashon Island. Seems I had not learned my lesson. I had a number of dances with a cute girl who was standing alone, but soon found out she "belonged" to a rather burly farm boy. There were some words exchanged, maybe a little shoving and soon I was at the bottom of the stairs and not about to return to the dance. There may have been alcohol involved. So much for small town dances!

I cooled it for quite some time; made several trips back to Seattle, on one of which Wilma dumped me for being absent too much and not having any transportation; I couldn't blame her. On another trip I found and bought one of my dream cars; a 1930 Model A convertible with a cut down top and Isinglass side curtains. It even had a manifold heater to warm the cab. I was in seventh heaven driving it back to Cheney even though I knew it was not the greatest car in a cold climate. (I still had not convinced myself I was in Eastern Washington) I found a garage so as to keep the car out of the weather, but failed to pay enough attention to the level of anti-freeze. (Permanent anti-freeze was not so available at this time) Went to start it in a few days only to find I had a cracked head. Bummer!! There are no parts in a small town, especially for an old car. I let a friend talk me into using the midnight auto supply; big mistake. It took about fifteen minutes to rip the cylinder head off some ones parked car and another hour the next day to install it on my engine. The following day when I test drove it down the main street I may as well have put a "stolen" sign on the car. Events do not go unnoticed in small towns. It only took a few hours for the local police to get in touch with me. I reversed the procedure, apologized and promised to be a good boy in the future. No one over reacted and having to return the item was punishment enough.

That little roadster that I truly loved was not to be the car of my dreams. I was able to make it into Spokane and finally found a used head. I put it on and replaced the anti-freeze, but apparently did not allow enough running time for it to mix with the water. When I went to start the car on my way to Seattle there were leaks in the radiator. I dumped in two bottles of sealant, crossed my fingers and headed for home. I was just short of Moses Lake when I ran out of water and the engine froze. I had a station in Mosses Lake tow it in, hitched a ride home and I drove back the next day in my parents car and a bumper hitch. (cars still had real bumpers) After I repaired the engine and radiator, my father convinced me that this was not the best car for east of the mountains. He also just happened to have a 1937 Chrysler business coupe, with both a radio and a heater that might just be a better fit. He convinced me!

I almost enjoyed returning to Cheney in a car that was warm, had twice as many cylinders as the Model A and was really fast. I stayed out of trouble, did my homework and did fairly well in school except for that stupid chemistry course. I drove home with Skeeter to Camas on a three day weekend where his family lived in a big house right along the edge of the Columbia River. I decided to test out one of his father's race horses on their backyard track. We hit the first turn, the horse went left, and the saddle and I went right; broken cinch plus a badly sprained ankle. I am a slow learner, for I would involve myself with horses twice more in later years and as of today due to apparent brain damage still own three.

I was really looking forward to spring break, for my father was to pick me up and we would drive to San Diego in a brand spanking new 1947 Dodge four door Sedan. We were to pick up my mother who was visiting her sister Lettie and then return home. We picked up highway 97 south through Washington and Oregon and then 99 at Weeds. We were finally getting into some warm weather. The highways were still all two lanes except in California where every few miles they would widen into three lanes, the center being for passing. My dad let me do almost all the driving and I loved playing chicken on those three lanes. I am not sure my father was as thrilled. It was exhilarating for me to get out on the highway and go fast; I am not really positive if there was a speed limit. We spent a few great days in one of my favorite cities and headed back home. At San Francisco we decide to go scenic and take 101 through the Redwoods up to Crescent City and then jog back on to 97. It was rather a nice drive up to Eureka and then the highway turned into a corkscrew with no way to escape. This is where the term "unimproved road" came from. My poor mother in the back seat had to hang on for dear life as we went around curve after curve for what seemed like hundreds of miles. We persevered and I was soon back at school for the final slog before summer vacation. What seems funny is that the one thing that stands out in my mind about the drive to California is a song. Many years earlier the band leader Ted Weems had brought out a song called "Heartaches." At the same time dad and I took our drive Weems brought out a new recording featuring the whistling of Elmo Tanner. For some reason it became a big hit and was always on the radio during the drive down and back and has since then stuck in my mind.

> Heartaches, Heartaches, my loving you meant only heartaches.
> —By; John Klenner & Al Hoffman

I felt that I had a chance to make it through till June. To the amazement of my Chem. teacher I actually found out what was in that clear vial. I received my life saving certificate and was passing math. Life was pretty good and even the weather was warming up and Skeeter and I could do some diving off the high tower at a nearby lake. Near the end of May two friends and I decided to make a last run to the state line and maybe to Coeur d' Alene. While we were at it we might as well have a beer at each road house on the right side going and the same returning to Spokane. In Coeur d' Alene fireworks were already on sale for the fourth so we decided to stock up. Idaho at that time had no restrictions on blowing yourself up, so there was some fairly heavy duty stuff available. We headed home hitting each tavern, but just drank small draft beers. We didn't want to get drunk, but I failed to realize just how many taverns there were near the state line. I remember throwing up at least once before reaching Cheney.

It was now a little past midnight, but before hitting the sack we felt that we should share our fireworks with all the other students thus saving them a trip to Idaho. We put on a nice show in front of each dorm and if we found an open door we would send a few screamers down the halls. Everybody loves those screamers. Of course we saved the best for last, a two inch in diameter aerial bomb. Boy was it loud; probably woke everyone in town and for miles around. There was a nice little man following us around whom I was sure was my friend, but I was to learn later he was the night watchman. In a few days we were brought up before the provost marshal who maybe gained experience prosecuting

German war criminals as it soon became obvious he did not take kindly to what we had done and let me know in a flurry of unflattering words. The decision of the disciplinary board was that I could finish the last few weeks of school, but would not be allowed to return in the fall. I was amazed; their decision matched my schedule exactly. Adios Amigos!

Was I ever glad to get back to God's country, work at S.L.Savidge, dance at Shady and get ready for rush and the University. Was this the end or was it the beginning? It was going to be touch and go getting into school as I came with a lot of baggage, but I just kept remembering that when you're out on a limb, the whole world is at your feet.

CHAPTER 17
DAM BUILDING

Up a lazy river by the old mill run,
That lazy lazy river in the noon-day sun
Linger in the shade of a kind old tree,
Roll away your troubles, dream a dream with me—

—Hoagy Carmichael

What is it that they say about the best laid plans of mice and men? Did I spend my summer at S.L. Savidge mucking around with new and used autos? NO! Did I go dancing at Shady Beach and hit their big water slide? Not till near the end of summer. What did occur had its start back in the early fall of 1945 when my friend Wayne and I decided to attend the last two days of the Pendleton Roundup in Oregon. Wayne had been invited to spend that weekend with his aunt and uncle who live 30 miles west of Pendleton in the town of Stanfield. Due to World War II the rodeo had been cancelled for 1942 and 43, but as the country began to feel more secure it was re-started in 1944. Even city boys knew the Roundup along with the Calgary Stampede in Canada to be the largest and most spectacular rodeos in the west. Wayne, being without wheels, needed me and we both were eager to see a big rodeo event. Having free room and board was the clincher.

The rodeo was everything it was advertised to be and more. The very first Pendleton Roundup was held September 29th, 1910 as a frontier exhibition of native Indians and the military along with demonstrations of roping, bronco busting and horsemanship from real working cowboys. It drew, what was at that time, an amazing 7000 people to the opening show. A huge crowd considering Pendleton was far from any urban center. Not much had changed by 1945 except that now up to 50,000 people attended and the contestants were more likely to be professional rodeo performers rather than working cowboys. Native Indians were still camped out in their teepees in every vacant area around the grounds. They represented the many tribes that once depended on the Columbia basin for their livelihood, but were slowly being forced out once more by encroachment of the "white man." I was surprised to learn that the Indian settlement a Celilo, some 116 miles west of Pendleton, on the Columbia River is the oldest continuously inhabited settlement in North America.

The nightly Happy Canyon dance and beer hall was yet another experience for boys not brought up on western dancing. I may have gotten in a Shottish or two as I recalled my early dance lessons from grade school, but none of the dancing resembled the Avalon. We made it back to Seattle late Sunday night; a nasty, hot drive over the barren Horse Heaven Hills, through Yakima, Ellensburg and on over Snoqualmie Pass, all on pre-freeway roads.

Forward now to 1947 and the Army Corp of engineers are about to start construction on the Umatilla Dam which had been in the planning stage since 1941, but had been delayed by the war. In 1945 it would be renamed the McNary Dam in honor of Senator Charles McNary of Oregon whom had died the previous year. By an odd coincidence Wayne's uncle in Stanfield, where we stayed during the rodeo, is helping to supply aggregate for the new dam. This was a huge contract, for the dam was to be 1.4 miles long with only the locks and spillways of poured concrete; the balance being packed earth and crushed rock. Wayne was assured a job by his uncle and he wanted me to come along (he still did not own a car) confident that his uncle would be able to find me a job driving truck as I had been a loyal, dues paying member of the Teamsters Union since I was 15 years old and had even handled a truck or two. He was convincing, so off we went at the start of summer, succumbing to the lure of making big bucks in dam construction. We were the eternal optimists as in this poem by an unknown author:

The optimist fell ten stories.
At each window bar
He shouted to his friends:
"All right so far."

It would, unfortunately, turn out to be one of my fantasies. It amazes me how naïve and un-worldly I and most teenagers can be, especially when they are so positive they know it all. First, Wayne's' uncle was not about to put me up in his house for an entire summer. I ended up in a large three story boarding house in the town of Hermiston, 20 miles west of Stanfield. Here I received breakfast and dinner plus a sack lunch to take with me to the job I was in hopes of getting. Sleeping was on an Army cot in the third floor attic. Second, reality struck when I went to get my truck driving job. There were no jobs unless you belong to the local unions. Hiring was done many miles away out of Pasco Washington and no one gave a dam that I was a Seattle Teamster. If a worker wanted to join the local unions he had better have two hundred or more dollars in his hand when applying. I was to learn this was standard practice on big construction jobs no matter where they are. I was beginning to feel out of place among these hardened professional construction workers that went from one big job to the next all over the country. There was not going to be big bucks for a kid. Wayne had it made helping around the rock crusher turning big rocks into small ones. I was on the outs, but was finally hired by Wayne's uncle as a flagman on the rail line that trucks had to cross getting to the big three story crusher. It was non-union so no big pay, but was required by the union for safety.

I was boarded in Oregon, but my job site was in Washington. Each morning our "rock crew" would assemble at the Umatilla ferry landing just below the dam where we were ferried across the Columbia River and then driven to the rock crusher and my railroad crossing. It's hard to describe the immensity of a dam project; one has to see it to believe it. We saw the work and progress every day as we crossed the river. A set of locks would raise boats 73 feet to the level of the future Lake Wallula Reservoir which would then allow ships access to ports many miles upstream that before had been blocked by rapids. The dam was unique in that two of the sixteen turbines would be used only to power dam functions, making the dam entirely self sufficient in case of a major disaster.

My mother and father with their usual insight had trepidations about my working this dam project, but in the end just let me work things out as best I could. They usually allowed me to make my own mistakes, but were there to catch me when I screwed up. Reminds me of a song by Van Morrison:

> When no one steps on my dreams
> There'll be days like this
> When people understand what I mean
> There'll be days like this
> When you bring out the changes
> Of how everything is
> Well, my mama told me
> There'll be days like this.

Remember the last scene in the movie "Castaway" when Tom Hanks stops his car at the crossroads, trying to decide in which of the four directions to go; as far as Hanks could see in any direction, nothing. That was me at my crossing post, nothing as far as the eye could see, just me and a small guard shack and a little red flag. I was fairly sure I was in purgatory and hell could not be far away. No way was a train going to sneak up on anyone as they could be seen and heard five miles away, but there was no red ding dong to warn drivers although I am sure they would have survived without my waving my red flag. Most of the time when drivers saw me waving the flag, warning them of a coming train, they just sped up to avoid the wait on a long train. I found it was best not to stand in the middle of the road when waving down a truck for fear of being flattened. The drivers loved to tease me and a few times were able to lure me onto the running board, grab my arm and drive off with me several hundred yards down the road. It did help break up the monotony of the day. I can only imagine what these drivers thought about this blond kid waving his red flag on a job they felt was unnecessary. All in all they were kind, good humored men trying to have a little fun teasing both me and Wayne.

I had my little guard house so I was able to get out of the sun, but there was no respite from the heat. In 1947 hats and sunglasses were not standard attire. It's a wonder that I did not die of heat stroke or go temporarily blind. During the summers in eastern Washington, as the land begins to heat up in the morning, it would bring with it a wind from the west which gradually increased as the day grew hotter until by late afternoon it became difficult to stand. Nothing blocked the winds path except my little shack, which at times barely remained upright. Occasionally a truck driver would take pity and bring me a cool pop. Each day was twice as long as it seemed and due to the pressure for more rock we would work on Saturdays. The pay was good for such an idiot job, but with time the money was becoming less and less important.

I usually saw Wayne only on Sundays as we lived 20 miles apart and I was too tired after work to make the drive. Instead, after work, I would head for a local tavern where I could have a beer and almost learned to play a card game they called Fan Tan. The influx of dam workers had caused the drinking age of 21 to be relaxed or ignored. I have no idea to this day what Fan Tan is or how to play it, which is probably why I kept losing money to these old codgers that played the game all day.

My friend Wayne was hardly what one would call a physical specimen. He was red headed, not large and had a pale white complexion to go with the hair. He was quite thin and had never been active in athletics. But, he was of good humor, kind, considerate and a gentle person, qualities often hard to come by. The men with whom he worked were just the opposite; big, strong, hard working, and hard playing and mostly single. After work they loved their beer and an occasional visit to our local house of ill repute that had, to everyone's surprise, sprung up at the same time as the dam project. These men loved to tease Wayne about his love life; especially after they found that at the advanced age of 18 years Wayne had yet to be with a woman. One night after plying Wayne with a few beers the men talked him into going to the "house" and having his sexual initiation. Wayne loved the experience and had a dumb smile on his face for a week, or up to when he visited the doctor's office and found that the reward from his little escapade was a dose of the clap. Thank God for the invention of Penicillin in 1940, just in time for our war wounded and Wayne. Prior to Penicillin the treatment was painful and rather gory. The incident proved to be no big deal and in some ways was like a red badge of courage to Wayne.

I was really beginning to dislike the job, the heat, the wind, those professional Fan Tan players and just the loneliness of being a crossing guard. I was, I decided, a people person, I needed to dance and swim and go out with cute girls. I needed to be kissed, to do the Avalon and ride that crazy rickety slide at Shady Beach. This was way too much like growing up and I was not ready for that. I think what finally pushed me over the top and convinced me to leave was the night the fan driven swamp cooler in the attic ceased functioning causing the temperature to soar to 120 degrees. When I had to spend the remainder of the night on the lawn fighting off mosquitoes I came to the realization that I was not cut out for dam building.

That weekend I resigned, turned in my red flag and said farewell to Wayne and my attic. I headed back to Seattle where the predominant color is green not brown. I readied myself for fraternity rush week, University registration and best of all spent a few Sundays at Shady Beach with some of the cute girls I had only been able to dream about.

> All the ways that lead to Somewhere
> Echo with the hurrying feet
> Of the struggling and the striving,
> But the way I find so sweet
> Bids me dream and bids me linger-
> Joy and beauty are its goal;
> On the path that leads to Nowhere
> I have sometimes found my soul.
>
> —From a poem by: Corinne Robinson

Post World War II led to the division of Korea into North and South. North Korea became a Soviet client state which in 1950 invaded South Korea who was backed by the United States and their allies. This in turn led to three more years of war and a heightening of the tension with the Soviets.

CHAPTER 18
DON'T PANIC—EPILOGUE

For I am not the guy who cared about love, and I am not the guy who cared about fortunes and such, never cared much , but look at me now.

—J. DeVries & J. Buskin 41

A s Yogi Berra said, "If you get to a fork in the road, take it." I guess I was now at that fork, wondering what had happened and what was about to happen. I was headed for the U of W, frat life and a futile attempt to rescue my engineering education. This would be my last summer for Shady Beach and the Avalon. The following summer I would drive to New York and stay over a month with my very first girl friend, Lilly Jean, and family. For me it was just a friendship visit, she wanted it to be something more, but it was not about to happen. I would not see Shady again as it was sold to King County and stripped of all its fun stuff, as was Lake Wilderness. Then again, Shady ceased being as important, as school and frat life came foremost. I kept a slender connection to the past by inviting old girl friends to functions so I had someone to dance with.

One time my pledge class had a sneak and I asked a high school friend Joanne J. as she was unknown to anyone in the fraternity. The sneak was a success and all the pledges made it to some obscure hall in the White Center district of South Seattle without being detected by an upper classman. (non detection was the object of a class sneak) The party dragged a little so they asked for volunteers to perform. Joanne was a trained acrobatic dancer and was eager to show her skills and other things. She did perform some amazing feats, all in a skin tight skirt. She was the hit of the party after doing a few back bends; at least with the boys. I think my image also went up several notches.

I sometimes wondered if there really was any point to life or as John Lennon had said, "Life is what happens when you're planning something else." It was Douglas Adams who asked, "What is the answer to life, the universe and everything?" In Adam's book, Deep Thought, the most powerful computer ever invented had mulled this question for 100 million years and finally came back with the answer; forty two. Makes sense to me!

So it's important to keep life simple and make the journey with just baggage enough. What we all hope for is that we can help make the world a good and happy place without having someone nailed to a cross. In a way my music and dancing became my religion. My sacred moments became my birth place, my first kiss or my first love. Vashon Island, the Arboretum and Shady Beach became holy places in my private universe.

Thank you for your time.

ACKNOWLEDGEMENTS

South to Java by: William Maek

Common Wealth by: Jeffrey Sachs

Wikipedia; the Big Bands

Minoru Yasui

Internet; The Big Band Broadcast, Letters from listeners

Glenn Miller Orchestra: A Tribute

Big Band Music: The Early Years

The Frank Sinatra Anthology by: Hal Leonard

Seattle Now and Then Volume I by: Paul Dorpat

Seattle PI: Story on David Thompson passing by: Scott Sunde

Seattle Times: Missing Son (4-10-45)

Seattle Times obituary 5-25-02 for David Thompson

Special thanks to:

George King	Gene and Maxine MacFadden
Sue Mucklestone	Bob MacFadden
Jane Morse	Jan Aszman
Dee Dee Hawley	Kim